Part-time courses in

Creative Writing
and Literature

Short courses:
online courses, summer schools, weekend lectures
and weekly classes

Oxford qualifications:
...rds and postgraduate degrees
Apply now for 2020 entry

D1016829

GRANTA

12 Addison Avenue, London WII 4QR | email: editorial@granta.com
To subscribe go to granta.com, or call 020 8955 7011 in the United Kingdom, 845-267-3031
(toll-free 866-438-6150) in the United States

ISSUE 150: WINTER 2020

PUBLISHER AND EDITOR	Sigrid Rausing
DEPUTY EDITOR	Rosalind Porter
POETRY EDITOR	Rachael Allen
DIGITAL DIRECTOR	Luke Neima
MANAGING EDITOR	Eleanor Chandler
SENIOR DESIGNER	Daniela Silva
ASSISTANT EDITOR	Josie Mitchell
EDITORIAL ASSISTANT	Lucy Diver
COMMERCIAL DIRECTOR	Noel Murphy
OPERATIONS AND SUBSCRIPTIONS	Mercedes Forest
MARKETING	Aubrie Artiano, Simon Heafield
PUBLICITY	Pru Rowlandson, publicity@granta.com
CONTRACTS	Isabella Depiazzi
TO ADVERTISE CONTACT	Renata Molina Lopes
	Renata.Molina-Lopes@granta.com
FINANCE	Mercedes Forest, Elizabeth Wedmore
SALES MANAGER	Katie Hayward
IT MANAGER	Mark Williams
PRODUCTION ASSOCIATE	Sarah Wasley
PROOFS	Katherine Fry, Jessica Kelly, Lesley Levene,
	Jessica Porter, Vimbai Shire, Louise Tucker
CONTRIBUTING EDITORS	Daniel Alarcón, Anne Carson, Mohsin Hamid,
	Isabel Hilton, Michael Hofmann, A.M. Homes,
	Janet Malcolm, Adam Nicolson, Edmund White

D.R.HARRIS & Co Ltd

—ESTABLISHED 1790—

CHEMISTS AND PERFUMERS

SPECIALISTS IN SOAPS, SKINCARE AND SHAVING SINCE 1790

---

29 St. James's Street
and 52 Piccadilly
020 7930 3915
www.drharris.co.uk

CONTENTS

Introduction

This is our 150th issue. Last year we celebrated *Granta*'s fortieth anniversary (in its current incarnation) by bringing out a special edition of some of the best fiction and non-fiction we have published over the years. Here, we celebrate language itself, publishing a range of authors who stretch writing to its creative limits. We take our theme from Pwaangulongii Dauod's remarkable eulogy to the late Kenyan writer Binyavanga Wainaina. 'There must be ways to organise the world with language,' Dauod writes, meditating on the explosive creative energy of Wainaina's vision for Africa. It's an apt title, given that all the fiction in this issue is visionary and dramatic, addressing existential themes and taking the space to do it.

Our opening story, by Carmen Maria Machado, plays with ideas of staged violence, visibility and invisibility, origins and renewal, a ghostly mirroring of a fictional pre-war Parisian theatre of pain.

Sidik Fofana's piece – a chapter from a forthcoming novel set in Harlem and written in American vernacular English – follows a schoolgirl sent South to stay with relatives over the summer. I've always been sceptical about writing in the vernacular, trapping characters in perceived idioms, but Fofana's writing is so inventive, and so persuasive, that you immediately lose yourself in it.

Che Yeun's story is about a South Korean teenager whose friendship with another girl culminates in violence. Can you survive outside the system? But then again, as a girl, can you survive within it?

Mazen Maarouf's 'The Story of Anya' portrays a teenage boy falling in love with a girl in a nameless setting where some people have special powers and dreams are sold for money. Like Elena Ferrante, whose psychoanalytic insights and thoughts order the world of her characters, Maarouf drops clues into the text. The story is punctuated with symbols from faintly familiar yet surreal settings: bulletproof glass, cancer, nosebleeds, signed bank notes.

After youth, midlife. Tommi Parrish's graphic story is about a ranting, middle-aged man at a bar who fails to connect with others. At the end of the story he is lying naked in his garden – I won't describe what he is doing there, but it's funny and a connection of sorts is finally made. This is a short chapter from a longer work about recovering addicts and other fractured characters – lumbering, gender-fluid people stumble through the pages; the dialogue is laconic, laced with gentle irony.

Perhaps the innocence of animals can be a salvation? Amy Leach's fictional lecture coaches animals to count, to become more professional (and more human), less hopelessly poetical and inefficient in their doings: 'Sometimes, when you see the emerald and ruby and sapphire sparkles on the snow, it seems like you are rich; sometimes it seems you can't get along without someone, seems the winter will never end, seems the moon is abnormally big coming over the mountains. But measurement dispenses with all the seeming: the bank account is low, the moon is normal-sized, etc.'

Other than Dauod's eulogy, we have three non-fiction pieces in this issue. Jack Kerouac travelled across America with Neal Cassady and others, an epic road trip described in his novel *On the Road*. Recently, Andrew O'Hagan told me about visiting Cassady's widow, Carolyn, who was living in a mobile home outside Windsor. I commissioned him to write this piece. 'They were just boys,' she says of Jack and Neal and the others. 'Just boys. But they had seen the sun together and that is everything.'

The second piece is also about old age. Photographer Michael Collins meticulously records the decline of his mother, who suffered from a series of strokes, gradually losing her ability to speak. His own terse language is perfectly in keeping with the subject matter; this is a sad story, and an important one.

Oliver Bullough, finally, describes what happened when a lawyer rewrote British Virgin Island company law, creating new channels for hidden money. Such is the power of language: words become law; laws change the world. ∎

Sigrid Rausing

THE LOST PERFORMANCE OF THE HIGH PRIESTESS OF THE TEMPLE OF HORROR

Carmen Maria Machado

I would never forget the night I saw Maxa decompose before me. I was a young woman, barely budded, but I'd been able to make my way to Le Théâtre du Grand-Guignol by telling my mother I needed to go to church.

My mother was a devout woman, a seamstress, and when I walked out the door she kissed me and said she was pleased I was seeking God's wisdom. When she pulled away I saw there was a black spot of blood where she'd brushed a pricked finger against the sleeve of my coat.

The entire way to the theater, a crow had fluttered around me. It fluttered from rooftop to rooftop, occasionally dropping down onto the cobblestones to fix me in its gaze before ascending again. Its eye looked like an onyx, and an oily prism blazed over its black feathers. My mother, had she seen it, would have told me the Devil was leading me. But she was not there, and she did not see that the bird could just as easily have been following me, as if I were the Devil. I kept walking, and it kept leading, or following, until I turned a corner and it ascended to a rooftop and disappeared.

The theater was built at the end of a narrow alley, lined with sand-colored buildings and pocked with shuttered windows and wrought-iron terraces. For a brief moment, the chatter of pedestrians fell away, and the Grand-Guignol glowed in the dusk. The cobblestones beneath my feet were the same I'd been walking on, but suddenly their unevenness made me aware of every rotation of my hip, every inversion of my foot. I felt like the theater took two steps away from me for every step I took toward it, stretching the space before me to an ever-doubling length.

The crow dove at me from a rooftop, shrieking like a djinn. I ran towards the threshold. The light pouring from the open door throbbed like a bruised thumb.

I had not, precisely, told my mother a lie. The theater had once been a church, though that night the room was hot with spectators instead of congregants, and just as cramped and feverish. The stage was claustrophobic, like a too-hot whisper from an intoxicated stranger. The cherubs that lined the ceiling had a demonic air, an askew quality, and seemed glazed in our collective oils. The smell of bodies was heightened – women's menstruation and the swampy folds of men. We all breathed in sync and through our mouths. I sat toward the front of the room, pressed between a man who kept glancing at me in confusion and desire, and a couple who gripped each other's bodies like they were about to be borne away by a flood.

When Maxa came onto the stage, it was as if a window had been opened to allow a breeze and a gale had entered instead. I felt the room bend around her. She was not beautiful in a traditional sense, but her dark eyes beheld all of us as if we were slightly familiar to her. Her mouth was painted the red of clotted blood.

The play concerned a wife who hatched a scheme to murder her husband so that she might live with her lover. Maxa played the strutting spouse with such assurance I forgot I sat shoulder to shoulder with my fellow Parisians; instead, I felt as if I were the play's maid, overhearing the strategic dialogue staged to divert suspicion. The plan was so nefarious, so meticulously plotted, I was certain I could reproduce it if I cared to. She turned to the audience from time to time, addressing us with scorn, sounding a little disappointed in our prudishness, our lack of imagination. We did not care. We arced toward her voice like petals to the sun.

In the final act, the wife lured her husband to her bedroom, where a large traveling trunk rested open on a length of oiled canvas. This was the plan: to murder him and pack him into the trunk, which she would take with her on a long journey. But before she was able to execute her plan, her husband seized the pistol and shot her dead. He wrapped her in her own canvas and placed her into her own trunk. It was heaved high in the air by an attendant and placed at the edge of the stage. The fiend murmured to himself – 'She thought of everything' – and then cackled as he walked offstage. Then, a tremendous bang, as the front of the trunk fell open to reveal her body, twisted in a grotesque knot. The audience let out a collective breath. A woman wept silently in the row before me, and her companion turned to console her.

I waited for the curtain to close on her death, but as I watched her body began to teem with a living curtain of maggots. Someone screamed – it was me, it was me – as her flesh blackened and greened and sank in around her bones like fallen cake. I felt like a girl-child trapped in a nightmare. Some tiny corner of me knew that the effect was done with something real – lights or clay – but could not convince any other part of me that this was anything but the end.

When the performance was over, I sat there picking at my skirt as the audience stood and shrieked and murmured confidences and eventually departed. I did not wish to return home just yet, while the nightmare of the performance lingered so close in my mind, and I felt warm and drowsy. No one came to move me, and I fell asleep there in my seat.

A slam, wreathed in whispering, woke me. The theater was dark as a tomb, aside from a candle burning in my periphery. I reached for my throat, as though I expected it to be wet or gone or bitten, but only felt my own rapid pulse. I turned toward the whispering and saw one of the confessional booths had been closed, and from within there was a gasping sound, like a woman being strangled. I stood and walked to the screen; pressed my face close. Inside, the dark-haired woman was bent over, a man rutting behind her. Her face turned to the side and she saw me, but instead of screaming, she pressed a white finger to the pillow of her mouth.

I turned and fled.

When I came back that night, my mother asked me what the sermon had been about. I went to her and admired her embroidery. 'The sinful Flesh and the living Word,' I said. She kissed me on the cheek. Her finger was still bleeding.

When my mother died of her wasting illness a few months later, I left our home – thrown out by the landlord, who'd asked for my body in lieu of rent – and found myself in front of the Grand-Guignol once more. I had some money on my person – enough for a few nights at an inn, a few hot meals – but still I turned some over for a ticket when I saw Maxa on the poster in the street. When I entered the theater, I saw once again the fleur-de-lys wallpaper surrounding me like so many seeds, like I was at the center of a large and pungent fruit – something unfathomably exotic.

That night, Maxa gouged out her right eye with a knitting needle. I don't remember why; all explanations and plot contrivances were weak beneath the weight of the violence. She dipped her head forward and her hand twitched with new weight. I thought it would be white and smooth as an egg, but when she pulled her hand away it looked like a stillborn chick; a round mass of wet and gristle. I realized after she let it fall to the stage that I'd been holding my breath, and the influx of air was sweet as summer rainfall.

At the end of the performance, I lingered near the stage, which was covered in gore. A young woman came out with a bucket and began to slop brown water along the wood. She looked up and saw me but said nothing. Feeling bold, I hitched my skirts and climbed up, stepping over a menacing streak of red. I could feel her eyes on me as I walked past her.

Backstage, Maxa was sitting on her chair, looking ravished. Her curls were already half undone, as if she'd been out on the water. A book was open in the dip of her skirts, and she was glancing at it with her good eye as she unpinned her hair. 'Sabine!' she shouted. In the reflection of her mirror, I looked wide-eyed, feral, faint as a spirit.

'Sabine, do you –' she said, and then flicked her gaze toward me. 'May I help you?'

Behind me, I heard footsteps, and the young woman, Sabine, appeared. She stepped around me and got very close to Maxa's face. Her fingernail scraped along Maxa's temple like a cat begging to be fed, and as the black peeled away Maxa's eyelid emerged beneath it.

'I'm looking for work, for room and board,' I said.

'Running away to the Grand-Guignol?' she said, her lips twitching slightly upward. 'This is not a place for children to escape to. Won't your mother be looking for you?' The effect seized the hairs on her brow, and she hissed a little. Sabine rolled her eyes, kept picking.

'I'm not a child,' I said. 'And my mother is dead.'

She blinked her eyes hard, the one that had been encased in blood blinking a little more slowly than the other. Then she turned toward me, her whole body leaning from its chair as if she were drunk. Did she recognize me, from that night many months ago? It was unclear. Her eyes were bright, as if with fever. I felt as if all the lights went out, they would glitter like will-o'-the-wisp and lead me into the darkness.

'Very well, Bess,' she said.

'My name is not Bess,' I said. 'It's –'

'It is now.' She hiked up her dress and pulled a flask from her garter.

Something – disappointment, maybe – flicked through the muscles of Sabine's face, but then it went flat, cold. 'Don't you have to ask Camille before –'

'I'll deal with him,' said Maxa. She lit a cigarette, stood. 'If anyone's looking for me, I'll be in the alley.' She tipped her head back and sucked at the flask as if it were a teat, and then stood and drifted into the shadows.

Sabine handed me the mop.

Even when the Grand-Guignol was empty, it was never empty. Fat mice waddled casually along the baseboards, searching for what had rolled out of view. We chased bats out of the theater daily, an explosion of fur and leather. Crows – maybe even my crow – took to sauntering in casually, searching for food or baubles left behind by terrified audience members.

Camille did not seem to understand why Maxa had hired me – though how could he, as I hardly understood it myself – but since I slept in her dressing room in the theater and Maxa fed me, he did not object. His round glasses did not stay on his nose very well; I offered to bend the wire, but he pushed them up nervously and turned away.

Maxa's vanity was cluttered with what she needed and more: bulbed bottles of scent with sleek lines, a small pair of scissors, mascaras and powders the color of chalk, lipstick and a metal tracer, kohl for her eyes, a hot curler, rouge, a fat brush tipped in pink dust, pencils, old scripts, a pair of bone-colored dice. It seemed like a place where spells were cast; that by scooping up a resident mouse and opening its throat into her wine glass, Maxa might be able to curse whomever she pleased. But there was no need for animal blood; powdered carmine arrived in small sacks – which Sabine told me was created by boiling insects – and I spent my waking hours mixing and reheating the concoction like a vampiress.

At night, before sleep, I stared at the ceiling and thought about my mother; the gap of her, the tenacity of her voice. Every so often someone would come to the theater's doors, rattle them with a drunken ferocity, and then their footsteps would recede. I understood better than most. I was outside those doors, once, but I never would be again. I could have been out on the streets, hungry and terrified. Here, the questions that seemed to have followed me my entire life did not seem relevant. I was invisible in a way that soothed me. My identity, my inclinations, my desires – it was all open for discussion.

Before my mother's death, when I performed the duty of pious daughter with rigor, there was a neighbor who often watched me from her window. My mother seemed to think of her as a useful eye

– keeping watch on our door when she went to the market – but the woman never seemed to be watching with anything besides curiosity and disgust. Once, when I played jacks on the stoop, she came out and stood at the bottom of the steps with a basket slung on her hip.

'Where is your father, child?' she asked.

'He's – no longer here,' I said, for that was what my mother said when 'dead' could not reach her lips.

She snorted as though she'd suspected as much.

'And who does your mother think she's fooling?'

I caught my ball and looked up at her face, hard with suspicion and even anger. I didn't know how to answer.

'We all know who she laid with,' she said. 'Look at you.' Then she shook her head and walked down the street.

A week into my tenure, I woke to find Maxa sprawled over her vanity, moaning into her arms. I stood, alarmed, and when she did not respond I rushed out to the theater, where Sabine was scraping candle wax off the floor.

'Maxa is ill,' I gasped, bent over from my pulsing heart.

Sabine stood with no tension, slowly wiping the blade on her skirt as she followed me backstage. She knelt down and looked at Maxa, who had fallen asleep.

'Wine or opium, Maxa?' she said loudly. Maxa moaned a little. 'Both?' Sabine said. Maxa slid from the dressing table and crawled into my cot. She was asleep before she finished her ascent, and her body went soft while bent over the wooden frame.

'Come,' Sabine said. 'If this is the new arrangement, you should know what needs to be done.'

We stepped into the sunshine and took off down the road. Sabine withdrew a novel from her basket and read as we walked. I could not see the cover, but when I tried to read the words she twitched and turned the book so I could not see. We didn't speak until we arrived at the pharmacist's, and Sabine located a blue bottle on the shelf. She shook it a little and held it up to the light.

'What is it?' I asked.
'*Recette secrete*,' she said.
'What?'
'Just some nonsense, but Maxa gets what she desires.' She closed the bottle in her fist. Her expression was flat and cross. 'Maxa watches you,' she said. 'She watches you like a cat watches a bird.'
'Jealously?'
She snorted. 'Hungrily.'
Back at the theater, Sabine lifted Maxa's feet up onto the cot and then dragged her torso upright against the wall. She slapped her lightly on the cheek, and Maxa moaned. Sabine handed me the bottle. I poured out the liquid with a trembling hand and lay the spoon against Maxa's tongue. She bit the metal and swallowed listlessly. Her eyes fluttered open and I felt like I was at the edge of the mouth of a cave, with every intention of jumping in.

After I'd helped Maxa prepare for the night's performance, I was allowed to sit in the audience, though not to occupy a paying chair. I thought I would become tired or bored of the same rotating sets of plays every night, but I could not stop watching Maxa. She exhibited control over every twitch. She never laughed when she might have laughed, never put a crack in the tension.

Every night, Maxa screamed onstage. Her scream was a magnificent thing, a resonating animal that climbed out of her throat and gamboled around the room. Some nights, if the room was particularly hot, I swore I could see the ribbons of her voice emanating from her. She screamed as she was raped and strangled, disemboweled, stabbed. She screamed as she was consumed by wild cats, shot in the gut, shot in the head (here, accompanied by an uncanny whistling sound, as if the scream was coming through the newly created orifice). She screamed as she was beaten, lit on fire. Audience members would stagger into the street to vomit, and at the end of the night the cobblestone street was studded with glistening puddles.

There were always a few doctors in the audience, sitting at the end of their rows. They were necessary, as fainting audience members were a regular occurrence. Mostly men, which caused a great deal of snickering and speculation among us.

The prevailing theory for this fact was that women were always afraid and covering their eyes, and men watched what they could not – and then found themselves unable to bear it. But Maxa knew the truth, and told me the reason for the fainting. Most men, she said, would only see bodily fluids when they caught their ejaculate in their hands, or if their life ended at the wrong end of a brawl. But for women, gore was a unit of measurement: monthly cycles, the egg-white slip of arousal, the blood of virginity stolen through force of hand or the force of law; childbirth, fists splitting the skin of the skull, the leak of milk, tears.

(I once saw a woman in the street who had been knocked about by a lover, or perhaps a customer. Her eye socket looked crushed; the new shape of her head made my stomach curdle. She was weeping but the salt tears were pink. She wiped them from her filthy face and looked at them on her hand: the color of a rare diamond. 'Even my tears bleed,' she said, and staggered down the street.)

'Men occupy terra firma because they are like stones. Women seep because they occupy the filmy gauze between the world of the living and the dead,' Maxa said. She was always saying stuff like that. But after watching her perform every night, I began to believe her.

Weeks and months, Maxa died again and again. One of them, in the early spring – death by slicing with a trick razor – was among the most dramatic I'd ever seen. I had watched the rehearsals but could not wait to see the final effect. Louis's forehead gleamed with sweat beneath the stage lights. He was more scared than Maxa, I realized. But then again, that was easy – Maxa wasn't afraid at all.

From behind the curtain, I glanced out into the audience. When I squinted, I could see that their collective foreheads were hazy with filth. When the curtains kissed, I glanced out again, and realized that all of their foreheads were crossed with soot – it was *mercredi des Cendres*.

I watched Louis slash thin lines across Maxa's breasts, blood seeping down her white slip. She shrieked in pain, her eyes glittering with pleasure. Then he drove the razor into her side. A stream of blood left her, as though he'd punctured a wine cask. The dagger's blade, I knew, sunk easily into its handle, and the blood I had mixed and warmed myself, but the effect was alarming nonetheless.

When the play ended, the audience went to its feet, and would not stop clapping until Camille told them to leave.

Backstage, Sabine staggered beneath the weight of her water bucket. She came up behind Maxa. The thin metal handle drew a white stripe across her red hand.

'I want Bess to wash me,' Maxa said.

Sabine flinched, and then dropped the bucket to the floor. Water sloshed on the wood and drew up what was dried there. I barely heard her receding footsteps.

Maxa slumped into her chair. In her hand she held her removed eye. I knelt before her and took it – a piece of chicken fat bound in twine and dipped in the carmine and glycerine, because the butcher had no beef eyes for us today – and set it wetly upon the vanity. I knew that the dark dip in her face was merely paint, but still when I approached it with a damp rag I felt something sour swell up inside me.

Maxa lifted her legs and balanced the balls of her feet on another chair. The fake blood had left dark lines down her body.

I rubbed the cleft behind her knee, not wanting to pull on the hair. She watched me, her lips pursed a little as if she wanted to moan but needed to stop herself. My rag felt like a living thing, a snake warmed by sunlight.

'My uncle was a garlic farmer,' Maxa said, closing her eyes. 'Hardneck garlic. Have you had it?'

'No,' I said, wringing out the rag in the bucket.

'It's wild and peppery – the best you can have. My parents sent me there one summer when they were worried the city was too wild for me. I would sit in the field and listen to the garlic grow. It sounded like a chorus of insects. I could hear a crackling, like onion skin. The air was green and sharp. They – they had such soft voices.'

Though outside the audience was talking, laughing, their voices were muted, as if the room were a womb.

'My uncle would harvest them and dry them braided together and hang them in bundles from the ceiling. The roots were like little hairs and the bulbs were purple as a man's eggs.' She laughed a little. 'My uncle would scold me, but sometimes I'd pull a clove and eat it raw. It tasted like –' Her mouth parted, in memory, and in her mouth her tongue glistened like an oyster. 'It tasted like a spell. When I got back, my father said I looked changed, and I think I was. I think the garlic tipped something in me. Kindling for a fire a long time coming.'

'Where is your father?' I asked.

Maxa opened her eyes, and her leg twitched beyond my grasp. She ran her hand along her thigh and stared at the pinkish water on her fingertips.

'Where is your father?' she replied.

I did not know what to say. She leaned down and took my chin in her hand.

'What was he? Maghrebin? Your skin is gold in this light.'

I flinched. 'I don't know,' I said. Maxa looked at my face like she wanted to bite it. Instead, she stood and examined herself. She seemed pleased. She walked behind me and gripped my shoulders in her powerful hands, and I felt blood rushing into the muscles that had been like stone. She worked her way around my flesh as if it were a spirit board and her fingers the planchette, drawing answers from my pain. I writhed and twitched beneath her. 'Thank you,' I whispered, but she was already turning away.

M axa's flat was a few streets over from Grand-Guignol, on the hill, in a rickety tenement at the top of a narrow staircase. She did not answer the door when I knocked, but the knob turned with no resistance.

Somehow, I had imagined a room bathed in light – a kind of temple. But it was closer to a courtesan's boudoir. At one corner of the room was a beautiful divan, with plush gold and red brocade and a single, sensuous loop of an armrest. The walls were hung with posters from the Grand-Guignol, a daguerreotype of a woman I did not recognize.

The shelf was piled with books, a tiny brass pot, a horsehair brush. An articulated mouse skeleton in a bell jar. Her bed was covered in a fur blanket, on which was draped a massive wolfhound. The dog glanced at me and growled a little, the muscles tensing and releasing in liquid bursts beneath her hide, but Maxa made a barely audible shush and she fell silent, her gaze fixed on Maxa's form.

'This is Athéna,' she said, gesturing to the creature. 'Hello, my little Bess,' she said. 'I'm glad you're here. I need to eat and bathe.'

When she let her robe drop to the floor, I finally saw the body that I'd only caught glimpses of. Her thighs were round, and the hair between her legs a rusty brown, through which the slit of her sex was visible. Her stomach had a low pooch, like she was early with child, and her breasts were small as apples. Thin white scars clustered near the clefts of her.

I drew a bath for her, and after she lowered her body into the water, I cut her meat pie into chunks and blew on them until they were cool. She wanted no metal, so I fed her by hand. Her mouth was warm and tight. She was careful not to bite but used the edge of her teeth to pull the meat from my fingers.

She let me sleep at her feet, near Athéna. Curled there, I felt the jabs of her toes as she got comfortable, sought pockets of warmth.

In my dreams, she walked down the streets of Paris on a winter night, and I followed behind. Green, waxy scapes pushed from between the fine hairs of her mink coat, and when the wind blew they rustled and, with a creak, reached further out. Her body blotted out the moon. She was an ambulatory garden, a beacon in a dead season, life where life should not grow.

S pring came. One morning, Maxa woke me from my cot by yanking my hair. 'I need you,' she said. 'There's a car outside.' As I stood, she undressed me – removing my nightgown and digging around in my trunk for a day dress. I stood shivering, my arms crossed over my breasts. When she'd finished, she unknotted my braid and gathered my hair into a soft chignon at the base of my neck.

In the car, our knees brushed against each other's, bone knocking against bone.

'Have you ever had your fortune told, Bess?' Maxa asked me.

I shook my head.

'I hadn't either, until I came to Paris. As a girl I had a doll who was meant to tell little girls' fortunes. She had a skirt made of slips of paper, and you would ask a question and open her skirts and there would be answers waiting for you. I consulted her daily. Once, I asked her if I was meant to be upon the stage, and when I unfolded the slip it said that I should give up, as evidenced by my doubt. So I shredded her little skirt until there was nothing left.'

I felt a terrible itch at my neck and reached behind to scratch it. My nails dug into the soft give of my skin, and I drew blood. Maxa leaned in and examined my fingers, dipping her own into the gore and examining what she found there.

'Many years ago, I visited a woman who told me many things that would eventually come to pass. But what happened after those events, she said, was shrouded in mist, and I needed to return to her once I met a *mulâtresse.*'

The car stopped at Rue Vieille du Temple, and Maxa paid and stepped out into the street. I followed her down the road, where carts stood pitched against buildings, and people of all types stood at low tables covered in fabric.

Maxa did not slow down at their tables; instead, she went to a particular door and knocked. A young girl answered. She tilted her head suspiciously up at Maxa, but Maxa handed her a small green stone, which she examined briefly. She shouted something in a language I did not understand into the house, and from its depths a voice answered back. Maxa pushed past the girl, who pocketed the stone and smiled at me, as if we shared a secret.

The room the girl led us to was dark and narrow, cluttered with bric-a-brac and a small table. The woman who sat at the table was young – perhaps the girl's mother – and she sat in front of a brass bowl and a glass pitcher filled with water.

'You've come back,' she said.

Maxa gestured toward me. 'I want the mist cleared,' she said. I sat in a chair in the corner of the room. A thin white cat leapt easily into my lap despite her ancient gait and rolled her skull against my breastbone.

The woman looked at me, her expression unreadable. Then she tilted her pitcher toward us and filled the bowl with water. She waited for it to settle, and withdrew a vial from her sleeve. A single drop of oil struck the surface, and after a moment it spread outwards. She cupped her hands around the bowl's edge and gazed deeply into it.

I looked over at Maxa. Her face had lost its lazy, indolent softness; she was alert, tense, her lower lip pinched beneath her tooth. The woman looked up at me again, and then returned her gaze to the water. 'You are a conduit for violence, but not a host. It passes through you,' she said.

'Is that all?'

'You will die a violent death.'

I saw Maxa gather the red tablecloth in her hands and feared she would yank the bowl and table over.

'Maxa,' I said, 'she's just a foolish woman.'

The woman's eyes snapped at me, and then drifted back down to her bowl.

'What do you see in there, about my friend?' Maxa asked.

The woman shook her head. Maxa dug into her glove and removed another franc. The woman slipped it into her purse and gazed back down.

'On a distant shore, your lover will find you,' she said. She looked back at me. 'What are you?' she asked, but I had no answer.

B ack in her flat, Maxa seemed agitated. She spun around, pinching the air as though reaching for something, and finally alighted upon a black box on her vanity. When she opened it, I saw soft spheres resting in between crumpled cloth. She removed one and held it up.

'A fig,' she said, 'all the way from Spain.' She handed it to me. It was warm and dense and heavy, and a milky drop of nectar clung to the fruit's opening.

'Where did you get these?' I asked.

'Oh, an admirer left them for me after a show,' she said. 'Eat!'

I did not know whether to bite or split, but Maxa bit into hers and I did as well. In the bite, I could see hundreds of tiny seeds, shadowed and clustered like orphans at an open door. I pushed into the opening with my finger, and the fruit clung to me like rugae drawing me in.

'It's the flower,' she said. 'It's grown inward, see? It is less beautiful but much sweeter for the effort. I'm told wasps crawl into its depths and die.'

The fruit slid down my throat, but I could not bring myself to take another bite.

I do not know when I first understood that Marcel was Maxa's lover; she never talked about him. Marcel was a queer figure, always fluttering and talking, the opposite of Maxa's languid substance. He was mealy and pale and perpetually damp; something one might uncover by inverting a stone in a garden. His hair was his only redeeming feature; long and soft. But I noticed that her chin twitched downward in his presence, and his never did. I did not like how he touched her, as if he owned her from her skin inward; the way he tangled his fingers in her hair and pulled as if drawing on a leash; and pinched her breasts and thighs as though testing her tenderness.

He did not like me either. He called me Maxa's little Arab, her whore, her *vase de nuit*. One evening, after the two of them had polished off a bottle of Arrouya noir, he put his cigarette out in my skirts. I yelped and leapt up from the divan, shaking the material so it did not catch on fire. From beneath heavy lids, Maxa watched this performance without comment, even when I looked at her for guidance. Then, she yawned, her tongue black with wine. Only the next day did she take me out to buy me a new skirt and laughed as if we were dearest and oldest friends catching up after an absence.

It was Marcel's idea to take us both to see *La Revue Nègre* at the Théâtre des Champs-Élysées. It was brand new, and nearly impossible to attend, but Marcel knew a man who knew a stagehand.

Maxa brought me to her apartment for preparation. The dress she'd found was short, heavy with silver beads, beautiful despite being shapeless. When I reached out to run my fingers through the fringe, Maxa slapped my hand away. 'Hair first,' she said, pushing me down in her chair.

Maxa let my hair down and tried to take a brush to it. The brush caught, resisted. She instead ran her fingers through from root to tip, lightly tugging at the snarls and knots. 'There's no reason to let it be like this,' she told me.

In the mirror, my hair made me look indescribably young. I looked away. 'It's always been this way,' I said.

'We should change that, Bess.'

'Why do you call me Bess?' I said.

She lifted my hair up like a curtain and let it drop over my shoulders. I thought she would refuse to answer, but when she spoke her voice curved with a smile.

'Have you read *The Highwayman*?' she asked.

I shook my head.

'A lover read it to me,' she said. 'He brought it from Scotland.' She fondled the curls that gathered around my ears. 'A landlord's daughter falls in love with a brigand, and he is betrayed to soldiers.'

She tugged again, and I yelped at the pain. She rubbed my scalp soothingly and then opened a drawer behind her. With a whisper, she looped a scarf over my wrist, binding it to the arm of the chair.

'Maxa –'

'The soldiers come,' she bound the other arm, 'and tie Bess – that's her name, Bess – to her bedpost, and place a musket between her breasts.' When she lifted the scissors into the air, I struggled against the bonds, but it felt perfunctory. I knew what was going to happen.

'She knows that they are plotting to kill her lover as soon as he returns, so she finds the trigger of the gun,' Maxa said. 'And her finger moved in the moonlight –'

The first cut was crisp and terrible.

'Her musket shattered the moonlight –'

Another.

'Shattered her breast in the moonlight –'

Again.

'And warned him with her death.'

I hadn't realized how much my scalp had been aching until so much of me was gone. My hair ended in a jagged horizon at my chin. 'I look like an urchin,' I said.

'I should leave you like this,' she said to my reflection.

I believed that she would, but then she laughed. 'I'm not finished.' She pulled the chair sideways and sat directly across from me, bringing the blade close to my face. Every dry snip sounded like a mouse setting off a trap. Dozens of snips, dozens of mice scuttling to their doom.

'So she died for her lover,' I said.

'He dies for her, too,' she said. 'At the end. He's shot down on the road.'

With the weight lifted, my hair gathered up into the curl I hadn't seen since I was a girl. She oiled it a little, then brought a hot iron to the ends, curling them under. After, she pasted curls to my forehead with petroleum jelly. 'Spit curls,' she said. 'One for every man you've kissed.'

'I haven't –'

'Shhh.'

'Maxa,' I said, 'are you still upset about the fortune teller?'

She shook her head as she dragged her finger down her tongue, sharpening the curl by my ear to a point. 'No,' she said. 'You're not a *mulâtresse*. That was my mistake. The reading was similarly in error.'

I stared at the tapestry behind her head – some Eastern cloth tacked to the wall; a tableau of tigers and elephants.

'What are you?' she said. 'Tell me.'

'I don't know.'

'What sort of an answer is that? You must know.'

'My mother was a teacher,' I said. 'My father died when I was young.'

A bobby pin scraped my skull and I flinched. Maxa looked slightly deflated, but then she busied herself at her vanity. She lifted up one of her bottles and poured out a spoonful. I opened my mouth obediently, like a child, and the liquid was bitter. I asked her what it was, and she did not reply. The powder puff huffed over my face, and I coughed. I felt a warmth gathering in my belly; the air softened. Maxa had been chewing on fennel seed; her breath was sweet.

'What country did your mother travel to, to teach the heathens?'

I closed my eyes, as if trying to remember, even though I knew I did not. 'A warm place,' I said. 'She was sent back after the war.'

'What do you remember, of the warm place?'

'Nothing.'

'Nothing?'

'Trees.'

'Don't be stupid, Bess. What kind of trees?'

I tried to imagine them, but as soon as one appeared in my mind's eye I saw my mother, laughing, bending down for me, and I felt my mouth tremble.

'Oh oh oh now,' she said. 'Never mind. Now is not the time. You have to be still.'

I clenched my anus and felt my organs settle in me. She drew on my face and it felt like she was drawing forever, like she was tracing my whole self because I'd faded away. Like I'd become a smooth dome of skin and she needed to put back what had vanished.

She lifted her gilded hand mirror and inverted it before me.

I did not recognize myself. My skin was pale as death, paler even, and the cupid's bow of my lips pouted unnaturally. My eyes were smudged dark as if I'd been struck twice. I felt old. Not as old as Maxa, nor as old as my mother before the illness took her, but old enough to have seen all of time in its infinite cycles, looping over and over again.

She unbound my arms and tossed the scarves back into a drawer. I lifted them and rubbed at the marks.

The dress Maxa had bought for me was oddly square – the style, yes, but beneath it my body's elements were subsumed. My new face sat atop a neutered body, soft and sexless as an infant's. I shivered, and Maxa produced her mink coat. The hairs grazed my skin and I had the uncanny sensation that a living thing was slung over my shoulders, breathing intimately against me.

Marcel came in without knocking, and he bent to the floor to gather the leavings from the haircut. He rasped them between his fingers with an expression of disgust before dropping them to the floor.

Then we were down in the street, and Marcel was opening a door, and a cab whisked us away. The car bobbed and weaved and jolted over the cobblestones like we were small and we were running and I could not tell if we were the escaping prey or the fox pursuing it.

Years before we arrived there, the Théâtre des Champs-Élysées had been the site of a terrible riot. I was a young girl but the stories reached my ears anyway: how Igor Stravinsky's *The Rite of Spring* alongside a ballet performance set in pagan Russia had set the audience to madness. They barked like dogs and climbed on their seats; I even heard that one of them tried to burn the theater to the ground. As we approached the facade, Maxa murmured something to Marcel, and he laughed raucously.

Inside, we took our seats, Maxa between us. The stage grew dark. From the ceiling, a platform descended, and as it landed on the stage I saw a woman, a Negress, sprawled on a bright mirror. When she looked up, I felt like she was staring directly at me. Her hair was slicked tightly against her head and the outline of her body gleamed like light on a river. When she stood, a set of long, pink feathers concealed her breasts and between her legs; she was otherwise nude. The music opened as a shimmer and then went wild; in the same way, the dancer began to jerk and turn as though seized with a fit. She seemed multiplied, three women dancing as one. And as she quaked, she sang. Her voice began low and wide and wooden and then lifted to the ceiling, bright and wire-thin. Between, it warbled as beautifully as any songbird. I felt something light up inside me like a candle knocked against a curtain.

'The Black Pearl,' Maxa whispered in my ear. 'Josephine Baker. They say she has a pet cheetah with a diamond collar.'

Around us, the audience leaned closer with every breath. They had, I thought, the same hunger as the Guignoleurs, though they didn't know it.

'Do you ever dream of singing and dancing, Maxa?' I asked.

The smile that came to her lips faded so quickly it was as if I'd imagined it. 'I only know how to scream,' she said. Marcel placed his hand on her thigh. 'And that's all anyone wants from me.'

M arcel knew a nightclub and hailed a cab for all of us. I had never seen so many different people in the same space. Parisians pulsed together, closer than I had ever seen in a street. Marcel vanished, and brought back two fluted glasses.

'What is this?' I asked over the music.

'Just drink it,' he said, turning away and gesturing to a man who seemed to know him.

'Maxa?'

'*Le soixante-quinze*,' she said.

'Why is it called that?' I asked.

The drink lurched as a man stumbled into my body, and then grasped the fat of my face in his large hand. He leaned in, inches from me. 'Because it is like being shot with a field gun!' he howled before Maxa pushed him away. Even as he stumbled into the crowd, I could see his glistening mouth and yellowing teeth; smell his rank breath. I closed my eyes and drank.

The drink bubbled in my mouth, an unexpected explosion of botanical sweetness. I drained it to the bottom, and Maxa handed me hers and gestured for more. Marcel lifted his own glass toward the jazzmen in the front. When he fumbled beneath Maxa's skirt, I looked away.

One young woman, a Negress with high cheekbones, danced with a white girl I'd seen in the Grand-Guignol many times. They held each other close, kissed each other's wrists, moved as if the room were empty. The familiarity between them made me ache. Maxa followed my gaze.

'Tomorrow they may pass each other in the street, and it'll be like they never met,' she said softly into my ear. 'That's always how it goes.'

'But they have what they want,' I said. 'Even just for a night.'

'Well,' she said. 'One of them, at least.'

We returned to the apartment in the earliest hours of the morning. Maxa gave me a glass of sherry, and I stared at it for a moment before crawling onto the divan and falling asleep. I heard her set it down on the nightstand, and the murmur of their voices.

I woke up to the sound of Marcel's open palm on Maxa's skin. With every crack, I imagined where his hand was going – her face, her buttocks – and when I turned my face ever so slightly I saw he was hitting glistening cunt. At every beat, she gasped and writhed, and tears leaked to her pillow. I closed my eyes, but the musk of her hung in the air and I could not make myself leave the room, even in sleep.

On a warm evening in May, Maxa invited me to take a walk with her. We drifted away from St Georges, down past the Théâtre Mogador. She held my arm with an uncanny intimacy, as if we had been friends since childhood.

'I have seen you write,' she said. 'Have you ever considered writing a play?'

'I've never written a play,' I said. 'I enjoy your performances, but I don't know if I could write anything that could rise to them.'

'It isn't about that,' she said. 'It's a pairing of power, not a transfer of it. The actress and the authoress meet in the middle.'

I picked up my skirts to avoid a pile of horseshit.

'You know,' she said, 'I like that you still wear this old-fashioned thing. I bet you still wear a corset, too.' I flushed.

'I only wear it because I can't afford anything new,' I said. She pulled me around another pile of dung, and when I was clear of it – but could still hear the buzzing of flies – she did not remove her hand but ran it along the line of my shoulder. I shuddered with the familiarity of the gesture.

Then we were at the Seine, past the Champs-Élysées, and I blinked at the river which had come up so suddenly. It flowed with an aggressive swiftness, and I suspected that if there'd been light in the sky, the motion would have made me dizzy.

'Have you ever noticed how the buildings become less crowded as you get closer to the water?' Maxa asked me. 'It's like the teeth of a young girl as she ages into an old woman. One day she has too many, and eventually she will have too few; a mouth of glistening gums.'

We began to walk over a bridge. Maxa turned to look out to the water. I did as well. The river unspooled before us like a line of spilled ink making its way across a table. Along the shore we saw something moving in the shadows.

'When I was a girl,' she said, 'a mad dog bit the neighbor's child. The dog was shot dead, but the girl became ill. My mother and I went to visit her, and in her bed she saw me and began to scream. She howled and kicked and acted mad herself, as if she would have rather torn through the walls with her bare hands than be in the room for one more moment with me.'

She fell silent, and I worried a chip of stone that had been resting on the railing. She did not say anything else, and after a few minutes we continued walking.

When we reached the nymphs at the center of the bridge, Maxa turned my body toward her. She bent my torso backwards over the cold stone and wrapped her hand lazily around my throat, like a sleepy man clutching his member to piss. Behind me, the black river was a starless sky, and the sky a star-filled river, and she pulled up my skirt and stroked my sex with her fingers. I hung there like a strung-up game bird, blood vacillating between my legs and my head, until I felt a swell like the air before a storm. My abdomen spasmed, and the more I trembled the more firm her grip became, and somewhere in the space between darkness and darkness my cells expanded outward and I bore down against her hand as if my muscle wished to vacate my skin.

'Thank you,' I said. 'Thank you, thank you.'

She pulled me upright and drew my shaking body against her breast. Then she kissed me as if extracting snake venom from a wound.

Back in her room, she removed her stockings and pulled her skirt to her waist. I went to her with my mouth, but she pulled my face toward hers and slipped my fingers inside. She circled my fingers, all muscle and fold, drew me in, and I moaned into her collarbone. It felt like I was pushing into a closed fist.

'Write me a play, Bess,' she said, panting and pushing against me. 'Write the filthiest, foulest, most tremendous play, and we will put it on.'

That night, I dreamt that I was spread-eagle on a ceramic platter larger than my body, glossy and white as the moon. In the sky, a blazing star grew larger and larger, coming toward both of us. Maxa sat down before me, and began to swallow me like a python, and I was gripped by the muscle of her until she'd taken me in entirely. The air grew white and hot and even as we were unmade, I was coming. When I woke up, nude and draped at Maxa's feet, I knew the play that had to be written.

'It's ready,' I said to her the first day in September. Around us, the cast gathered for rehearsal. Maxa took my face in her hand and kissed me, long and slow.

'Wonderful,' she said, her mouth twisting up into a smile. 'I crave the experience of reading it next to you. Wait for me after tonight's performance, and we will read it together.'

That night, I let myself in and sat on her bed, the play resting on my lap. The show had recently ended, and when enough time had passed for Maxa to change, I expected to hear her footsteps on the stairs, but there was nothing. Athéna chewed on a cow's bone in the corner, but after a while she ambled up to the bed and laid her silky head on my lap, on top of the pages. As the hours wore on, my back became stiff, and I drifted into shallow half-dreams until my wilting body woke me with a jerk.

Well past midnight, I heard voices on the stairs; Maxa's sotto, Marcel's reedy as a girl's. When the door opened, I saw Maxa's surprise soften into remembrance. They were both drunk; a haze of anise surrounded them. Athéna growled lightly at Marcel.

'Your little dog is here,' he slurred at her, and I realized he did not mean Athéna. He walked up to me and grabbed my knee through my skirts. 'Will you service us both? Or are you as useless a hole as you are an attendant?'

'Marcel,' Maxa said. He turned and grabbed her wrist.

'What, my love?' he sang, his voice shot through with threat. Athéna barked, a ridge of fur raised along the back of her neck.

She twitched and twisted her arm away but said nothing else. Marcel looked at me again, and while arousal was in there, somewhere, it was mostly anger. He kissed Maxa gently on the cheek. She did not look at him.

'Goodnight, my queen,' he said, and left.

Maxa stood there in the darkness of the room. I could not see her face. I thought of a doll I'd had as a child, a faceless doll my mother told me had come from my grandmother. A young girl who lived nearby drew a face on my doll in charcoal, and after that I would not touch her.

'Bess,' Maxa said finally. I stood there, the pages tight in my arms. She tried to take them; after pulling hard, I relented. She sat on the bed and flipped through them, reading with the kind of sustained focus I normally only saw on the stage. When she arrived at the climax, her eyes glittered. 'Oh Bess,' she said. 'Bess, my Bess.'

I got down on my knees, but she drew me up and laid me on the bed. 'I am so sorry,' she said, stroking my hair. 'I am sorry for Marcel.

He's a slug and a bore, and you're like lightning that turns sand to glass.' She rubbed her thumb over my pulse.

'Why do you stay with him?' I asked.

'You're so young, Bess.' She lifted my skirt with a rustle and leaned her mouth into my ear. 'You simply don't understand. The world is terrifying for women. For us.'

She began to massage my sex with her thumb, and when my body acquiesced she slipped inside. Her thrusts were saturated with need, as if her hand was a cock. I whimpered and felt myself curl around her, and she sealed her free palm over my face. 'Bess, Bess, my little Bess,' she whispered. 'Do you want to go to Greece with me?' Her hand did not move from my mouth. 'We could leave this theater and take a train to Thessaloniki. We can tell people we're cousins and no one will pry. We can have goats and sheep and plant garlic and we'll never have to labor outside our own walls.'

I felt pleasure from far away, like a horse cresting the horizon. The door to her flat rattled loudly, and Marcel's slurred voice drifted in from behind it.

'Maxa,' he said. 'Maxa, come with me.'

My back arched, and she pressed her hand against my mouth. The sound that had nearly escaped moved back and forth between my cunt and my head, with no release.

'I come to you, my king,' she chirruped bright as a bird, and then whispered in my ear, 'I will check the train schedule, I promise.' She slipped her hand out of me, whisked her coat around her body, and was gone.

When the door shut, the sound that had been staggering through my body came out in a ragged sob. The candle on the table guttered, even though there was no wind.

The troupe gathered to read the play together, and when it was over a pall of silence descended onto the room.

'This play is profane, even for us,' Sabine said. 'The police will come.'

Camille looked helplessly at Maxa, but she was smiling at me.

'Don't be afraid, loves,' she said. 'This is going to be the best show we've ever performed.'

The night of my play's debut, I arrived at the theater early, only to find Maxa and Marcel drinking on my old cot.

Maxa's eyes glittered. 'I've had an idea, Bess,' she said. She lifted up a cigar box and opened it; inside were lines of francs.

'Maxa,' I breathed.

She sent me down into the house to place the bills on the seats. I did, and when I had leftovers I turned and showed them to her. She made a scattering motion, so I swung around and released the bills everywhere. When I had rid myself of every scrap, I returned to the stage and to the peephole where Maxa stood.

The audience began to enter. The Guignoleurs moved with swiftness, and others flinched and rolled their eyes upward, taking it all in. Then, a woman in a beaded dress noticed a franc on her chair and lifted it to her eyes. She turned to her companions, who were laughing. 'It's real!' she said. 'It's real!'

Her musical voice ran through the crowd like a swift illness. Others began to echo her, unthinkingly at first, and then it took as they saw the paper scattered at their feet.

'Let me see,' said Maxa.

Marcel, Maxa and I stood there, taking turns at the peephole. Maxa laughed wickedly, and when Marcel looked I saw his muscles tense, like a cat about to pounce.

'Please,' I said, and pressed my eye socket to the peephole.

In the audience, the patrons tore at each other. The ladies abandoned their hats and handbags, crawled over each other, their skirts riding up. The men punched each other in the jaw, cracked chairbacks against skulls. They did not look human, but rather like a group of feral cats I had once seen swarm over a horse who had fallen in the street; liquid and animal.

Maxa's breath was hot in my ear, and I felt her pressing against me. It was only when the pressing became rhythmic that I realized that Marcel was behind us both, and Maxa's skirt was drawn up to her hips. My breath quickened, and I braced myself against the wall, so that I might slip away. Maxa grabbed my wrist.

'Please don't leave me,' she begged into my ear. 'Please don't.'

A woman who had been rummaging about on the floor sat up, a fistful of francs in her hand like a wedding bouquet. But instead of pocketing it, she threw it back above the crowd, refreshing the chaos. I heard Marcel make his groan of culmination, and then he was gone, disappeared into the back of the theater. I turned around and saw Maxa there, looking disheveled. Sabine came running up to us – 'Maxa, you need to change!' – and then I went and sat in the audience.

And so the play began.

I had, as Maxa commanded, written the most degenerate play I could have imagined.

Jean walked to the center of the stage. 'I am your host for the evening. Tonight, we will not be showing *The Blind Ship*. Instead, we have the debut performance of a new play, by a playwright brand new to our stage. A virgin, if you will. The play is called *The Star*.'

The audience tittered. Jean lifted his arm and walked to the edge of the stage, bowing as he did so.

'The village of Roquebrune-Cap-Martin,' he announced, 'at the end of the world.'

When the curtain rose, Maxa was standing atop a swelling slope, a falcon on her arm. Behind her, a servant lifted bits of bloody meat to the falcon's beak, which the falcon seized with a quickness. Beneath the stage, attendants used water and mirrors to send soft and glittering orbits into the room, as though she stood on the ocean's shore. She smiled. Her lip curved like a hooked finger drawing a viewer into a room.

'It is the end of the world,' she said. 'See, the comet in the sky. It tears down toward us, threatening. I am the last queen that reigns over man.'

Jean dropped to his knee. 'I would do anything for you, my queen.'

'A comet in the sky,' Maxa repeated again. 'I thought it was the moon, but it is coming to end us. It bears down on us like a disapproving eye. It reveals truths and dispels illusions. It causes us to remember what we never knew we forgot. It causes us to forget what we never knew. We are small, we are small. Mankind's theater is wasted on our smallness.'

We arrived at the part of the play where the dialogue and stage direction ceased. The actors were instructed to turn to the audience.

'What do we do with our final queen?' they said, in unison.

There was silence among the audience. I waited for five breaths before opening my mouth to command: 'Worship her.' I imagined an orgy of bodies. Indeed, even Jean was unbuttoning his cuffs, preparing for the audience's lust.

But in the same instant, a deep voice bellowed from the crowd, swallowing my own. 'Strike her down.' There was a beat of silence, and the actors did not respond.

Another voice, higher this time. A woman's. 'Subdue her.'

'My people,' Jean said, rolling up his sleeves. 'The comet arrives. The end of the world is nigh. Perhaps . . .' He flicked the edge of Maxa's breast suggestively. Beneath the fabric, her nipple hardened to a pebble, but she did not move. She continued to stare at the audience, impassive, her face slack as dough.

'Beat her,' said another man.

Jean looked at me, but I did not know how to intervene. My play felt alive, less created than born, and I had no more control over it than any being.

The first blow was soft, like a parent wishing to frighten a child instead of hurt them. Maxa barely moved; the hand seemed to sink into her. Jean turned back to the audience, a troubled expression moving across his face like clouds before the moon.

'And now that she is softened,' he began, 'perhaps we –'

'Again,' said a young woman, who barely looked old enough to be in the audience.

Jean looked at his hand as if he did not recognize it; as if it was some creature that had climbed onto his limb for a ride. He struck Maxa again but did not look at her.

Now the audience was silent, but the command rose from them like a collective thought. Their white faces bobbed in the blackness like so many corpses in the river. Jean hit her again, and again. As she fell, the falcon took off from her arm and swooped toward the woman with the scraps of meat. She shrieked and tossed them to the ground; the bird landed and swallowed them one after the other.

Jean grabbed Maxa's hair and lifted her to her feet.

The fifth time he struck her, a woman stood up in the audience. 'Stop!' she screamed. Around her, a few glazed eyes turned upward. She grabbed the jacket of her escort, a dewy young man who looked at her as though she was making an observation about the weather. 'Stop,' she cried again, and stumbled over the legs of audience members so that she might make her way to the aisle. 'He's hurting her, he's truly hurting her!' she said, pushing over the bodies in her way. 'Make him stop!'

Jean struck Maxa again, so hard I heard a crack and she collapsed to the stage for a final time. The woman kept pushing her way through the audience, and in one swift motion a group of men stood and bore her body aloft. She shrieked in fear, and once again cried 'Stop, stop, he's hurting her!' and the men passed her back, and men and women alike pushed her into the air, her body contorting like a puppet, and they passed her around, pulling the clothing from her like the skin from an orange. Segment by segment, her garments fluttered to the floor. Her body was white as pith.

She began to scream anew – no longer for Maxa, but for herself. The actors stood there, waiting out the stage direction that had so delighted Maxa: *When worked into a frenzy, let the audience play out their desire until their exhaustion and natural submission.*

Then the crowd opened up like an orifice and drew the woman into itself, and she sank as if in quicksand. There was a sound; a slurping, a yawn, as if she had entered into a giant mouth. Then as suddenly as it had begun, the audience returned to their seats. The woman was nowhere to be found.

Jean's eyes were soft and wet as rose petals. He staggered past his cue. 'It comes,' he said, though what was coming he did not say. 'It comes.'

The effect of the comet striking the earth was twofold: light and sound. When the stage cleared, the actors had dropped down flat, and the falcon continued to eat, a hard eye turned to them all. Of course they should have been nude, having fallen directly from whatever sexual position they'd been imitating. But instead they dropped from violence to death with nothing in between.

The audience sat there, as in a trance. Then, they began to clap, and clap, and they stood. Cloth from the woman's dress was strewn over the seats and their arms, and they clapped and clapped and clapped. It was only the lights coming up that stopped them from clapping unto blood.

Camille met me backstage. 'We will switch back to *The Blind Ship* tomorrow,' he said. He pushed a pile of scripts into my hands.

When the audience had departed, I walked up the sides of the aisles, looking for the woman. I saw white scraps of dress, but no naked, crawling thing, not even a corpse. I walked the perimeter of the theater, but she was simply gone.

M any years later, when Paris was a distant memory, I asked myself if I had known that the audience would not encourage the actors to descend into an orgy, but would instead demand Maxa be taken apart before them? That only the intervention of a woman in the audience, a stranger who then lost her life at their hands, had prevented such a thing? I did not know.

W hen I arrived at Maxa's flat that night, I found Athéna looping around the street, whining piteously.

I ran up the steps to the flat and leaned my ear against the door. Marcel's reedy voice floated toward me. 'I love you, my demon, my sweet,' he said. I heard the sound of leather on skin, but was not certain if it rang with rage or pleasure. The cracking sound ended with the faintest of chimes – metal. I began to throw myself against the door.

'Bess,' Maxa screamed from inside. 'Bess, help me, help me please, God help me.'

As the door gave beneath my shoulder, the belt buckle struck the side of my face. I spun blindly and pinned Marcel to the wall, yanking the belt from his hand. I struck his groin, and he crumpled.

'Get out of here,' I said. He stood and ran.

I closed the door and turned back. Maxa was sprawled on the divan, weeping. Her dress was torn, and welts bubbled on her skin as if she'd been burned. I wetted a cloth with water and brought it to her.

'Oh Bess,' Maxa said, clutching tearily at my skirts. 'He was mad, he was mad. I did this, I lit some wicked fire in him. He wished to purge my sins –'

'You'll be all right,' I said, dabbing at the welts.

'I lit some fire in you, too. I created you, turned you into a monster.'

I lifted the cloth and let it drip onto the floor. Maxa gathered herself from her weeping and stared at me as if she did not recognize me.

'I am not a monster,' I said, 'and you did not create me.' I confess here that my voice wavered a little, for I thought of my mother, and for the first time in a year longed to hear my name, my true name, in her voice.

Maxa laid her head against my stomach as if she were an exhausted child. I stroked her hair. 'You love me, don't you, Bess?' she asked. She looked, the goldfish of her mouth trembling. She smelled like *le fruit défendu*, like overripe apricots fallen to the earth, bitter smoke. I held her face in my hands; it was lovely and cold. 'I must go,' I said, and she did not stop me.

I opened the door, and before I left whistled for Athéna, who loped up the stairs and went straight to her mistress.

The next morning, Maxa was gone. No one at the theater knew where she was, though she'd left a note, and Sabine was preparing to fill in. Marcel, they told me, had been arrested in the night for his drunkenness – he'd assaulted a woman outside a hotel after he'd left Maxa's flat. An officer lingered in the doorway, after having made inquiries about a disturbance, and a young woman who had not returned to her dormitory.

'What kind of theater is this, exactly?' he asked, squinting nearsightedly at the poster on the wall.

'We perform religious plays,' I said breathlessly. 'Excuse me.'

When I arrived at Maxa's apartment, I found it full of her possessions and empty of life. It was only when I asked her landlord that he procured a piece of paper with her thick, cramped handwriting – a forwarding address in Rouen, and several months' rent. I caught the next train.

When I arrived, I hired a driver. A steady rain obscured the details of the landscape except for the turning of the wheels, and the road unfolding behind us.

It seemed like an age that I stood at Maxa's door, my wet hair wrapped around my throat like a noose. The yard was quiet as a cemetery. Beneath a willow tree, loose soil bulged with new death. A shadow slipped across the window, and I knocked. She did not answer. I threw myself against the entrance, but slipped and fell into the mud. I stood and lifted a stone, intending to break the lock, and the door opened. I saw a single, liquid eye. She opened the door further and took me in. She looked at me as if she'd never seen me before. I pushed past her and into the warm little villa.

'What are you doing here?' she asked me. She looked frailer than I remembered her, wrapped in a blood-red kimono lined with blue and gold cranes. She turned toward her window, and then her eyes seemed to land upon the grave in her yard. 'Athéna died. Her back legs went soft and she shit herself and then she left me in the middle of the night. Sickness follows me wherever I go.'

My jittering fingertips missed the buttons before they found them. I undressed before her and pressed her hands against my gooseflesh.

I thought they would be warm, but they were cold, even colder than me.

'Strike me,' I said.

She stared at me as if I were mad.

'No,' she said.

I grabbed her hands and placed them around my throat. When I released them, they fell limply to her sides. Water dripped down my body.

'You asked me if I loved you.'

'I –'

'I don't need you to tell me you love me,' I said, 'but you do need to tell me that I will not be limping after you for our entire lives. That my humiliation is not your only pleasure. I don't want your performance or your persona. I just need to know that you need me, or some part of me.'

Her eyes filled with actress's tears, and when my face did not soften, they sharpened into real anger. 'Need you for what,' she said flatly. 'I'm not an invert.'

The slap I delivered to her cheek was not hard, but she crumpled to the floor like a kicked animal anyway. There, I heard a high, keening sound, and I realized that she was weeping. I had never heard her truly cry before. She clawed listlessly at the wooden floor, as if it were earth and she could bury herself there. I pulled up my dress. She stayed on the floor, curled into herself. I would never see her stand again.

'I'll find you, Bess,' she said. 'On the distant shore, remember? I will find you, when I can be better than I am.'

'My name is not Bess,' I said, leaning down to her. 'And you will never know what it really is.'

As I walked back to the train station, the rain began to dissipate, and the clouds faded like breath dissolving into the winter air. When I arrived at the station, the bustle of it was strangely muted. I looked up into the sky. A bright new star glittered next to the waning moon, and the people on the platform pointed to it in wonder; faces all turned equally toward this new sight.

Watching the countryside flit past the fixed window, I remembered something I hadn't thought about in a long time: the first time I saw Maxa, decomposing on that stage. How she had let herself dissolve away.

I drifted west, to London, where I worked as a seamstress like my mother had and spent what little discretionary money I had on the movies.

I loved silent films – perhaps because of the dark eyes and expressive faces of the actresses, which commanded with so little effort – but when sound arrived I felt a fluttering moth of excitement. The world was advancing forward, in its own way. I did not know then, sitting there in the darkness, that under the dialogue I was hearing the death knells of the Grand-Guignol from across *la Manche*, one pleasure traded for another.

Then the war came – men doing what men did. When it was over, and the newspapers were filled with humankind's unspeakable horrors, the Grand-Guignol no longer had anything new to show us.

I emigrated to the United States a few years before Hitler's occupation of Paris. My life settled into some manner of routine. Montmartre was in my past and would remain there.

One afternoon, a letter arrived for me from Algeria: my aunt, searching for me.

'I have sent a dozen letters after you,' she wrote. 'Many years have passed since we have laid eyes on each other. It was terrible to lose you, beloved creature; I hope to find you soon.'

The letter was soft from its travels and, when I placed it against my nose, smelled like incense. My mother had dabbed an oil onto her wrists when she was alive; at night, always after I'd gone to bed, though it lingered on her in the morning. It smelled like this, like a fire in a cedar grove. I had not smelled it in so many years. My body seized up with distant grief, and that was how my lover found me – sitting in an armchair and clutching the letter to my breastbone, spasming with anguish. She brought me a pen and the stationery with my name embossed at the top. 'Write back,' she said.

The next afternoon, as I carried my letter to the post office, I felt something on my neck – the sensation of Maxa's gaze. Though she was decades past, I flinched and reached up to smooth the hairs that had prickled there. I turned. It was a bright, matte day. The sky was the color of strangulation; the streets glittered like crushed glass. Beneath them, New York's creatures teemed and strutted like they'd all been loosed from their circus.

Then I saw her face, looming up from the cover of a magazine. The vendor who was selling it smiled toothily when I handed over my money.

At home, I spread the magazine open on the table. I AM THE MADDEST WOMAN IN THE WORLD, the headline read, and what followed was a first-person account of what Maxa perceived to be her life. I read that she had returned to Paris after her time in the country, and of the series of doomed love affairs she'd carried on then. One man, a Parisian businessman, had made her line the walls of her flat with black velvet. I pictured her on the bed, curled up there, like a tiny brooch at the bottom of a jewelry box. She had, it seemed, returned to the Grand-Guignol for a final performance, in which she screamed so loudly she ravaged her voice, and could now do nothing but whisper. The article did not mention me, except for a single reference to the 'degenerate women' she had power over.

My lover read the article over my shoulder, her breasts grazing my back. She did not speak as I flipped the pages, only huffed a little through her nose when she arrived at certain lines. When I was finished and set the magazine down on the table, she said, 'Come, my little degenerate, let's go for a walk.'

When I didn't move, she slid her fingernails along my scalp and gripped my hair at its base. When she gently pulled my head back, she delivered a kiss to the naked arc of my throat. I felt a spasm of joy.

'Now, Aisha,' she said into my skin, her voice acid and sweet, and my skull vibrated with my name. I stood and followed her into the street. ∎

Carolyn Cassady at Mills College in Oakland, California, where she was training in occupational therapy, 1945
Courtesy of Neal Cassady Estate

CAROLYN

Andrew O'Hagan

C arolyn's past was preserved in amber. She'd had a decently long
life – children, lovers, hairbrushes and old mirrors – and she
trapped the paraphernalia, stacking it on shelves and into bureaus at
her tiny attic flat in Belsize Park. I never asked her how she ended up
in London, she was a Denver girl, by way of Michigan and Nashville,
Vermont and California, although she told me she'd always been a
fan of 'the miles between' and 'the long and winding road'. She wore
old-fashioned perfume, which turned out to be Chantilly. I imagined
it was like a scent from the 1950s, her best years of being pretty,
though she was always pretty, and when she opened the door to me
she beamed in her old-lady specs and said today was as good a day
as any.

Her blonde hair was up in clasps. She wore white slacks and a
plaid shirt, with a knitted lilac vest over the top. She asked me if I
wanted a 'drink-drink', but it was too early for that so she boiled
the kettle and we sat by the window. I tried not to think of her as a
woman surrounded by the male ghosts in her life, but I'd come to
speak to her about Jack Kerouac and her husband, Neal Cassady –
who inspired *On the Road* – and the air was thick with those men and
their inexhaustible legacy. I was young at the time and she told me
I reminded her of the democratic souls with whom she'd misspent

her youth. 'Any level of society, Neal was comfortable with,' she said. 'Both of them were the most compassionate men I've ever run across.' She showed me some letters and looked towards the window. One of the letters was from Kerouac to her, talking about Allen Ginsberg (whom she didn't like very much) and the other was a letter typed by her husband to Jack, dated 17 December 1950. I think she'd retyped the opening. She didn't mind me copying out a few sentences. 'I earned but 180 bucks in the last 5 weeks,' it said. 'The fixing of the car for east trip is proving well nigh impossible. If I must travel by train, transportation of tape recorder big problem, but on the soul of death I vow to have you and this fragile instrument wedded within the month. I must tomorrow find job here in SF to get money for trip. Carolyn is about to starve, as is Diana. Poverty looms big.'

She turned to me. 'Jack finally began to realise he would never be a husband and father, although he talked about homes with me all the time.' She spoke for an hour or so about Neal's imprisonment and Jack's decline, the way it all fell apart. 'At the end of his life, Jack would make these late-night phone calls to me,' she said. 'He said horrible things. Things you shouldn't say to a woman. He was only forty-seven and it was too sad. I tried to make a home. But is any home the right one, and do they ever last the way we would want them to?'

You Can't Go Home Again. I thought of the title of Thomas Wolfe's great novel, a sweeping account of a writer's life in America. It was a favourite of Jack Kerouac's when he was young and it influenced his own journey out. That afternoon with Carolyn felt like the beginning of a good friendship, but I disappeared, we both did, into our families and our trials and the various tasks that seemed so important at the time. I would often see her from my office window on Haverstock Hill as she shuffled past Budgens, and one time I ran down in a T-shirt with a pencil still lodged behind my ear, but she was gone. After a few years I stopped seeing her at all and wondered where she was. Ten years passed, then another five, during which a lot of people disappeared and I began to hover over my address book, wondering whether crossing out their names was an act of violence against them.

One day in January 2013, I woke up feeling I wanted to see Carolyn. I had no idea where she was and there was no answer at her old number. I went through a television producer and eventually discovered that she was living in a mobile home park near Bracknell, not far from Windsor, and I wrote to her. I wasn't sure she would remember me or that she'd be in the mood for visitors, but she wrote back pretty fast to say she hardly saw anyone and hadn't been well but was up for a visit. It took a few days to organise. We were soon in contact by email, which she used like carrier pigeon. She had the gasman coming ('The Gasman Cometh!') and gave me details about how her mobile home was heated and how it broke down all the time. She said she might send another email tomorrow. Eventually it arrived, speaking of Walt Whitman and how the sun was out.

Carolyn felt uncertain about the ability of my car to reach Bracknell. 'Do you know how to find me in this maze of a Mobile Home Park?' she wrote. 'I can give you hints if needed. The little gizmos on your dash won't tell you enough. Looking forward. (Sun today!!) Carolyn.' In London that morning, I parked my car at the National Theatre and went to a meeting. Having promised Carolyn lunch, I then walked over to the deli counter at the Delaunay to pick something up. She said she liked pickles so I got two bagels with salmon, cream cheese and pickles, and, while I was at it, had them box up two German cakes featuring pineapple.

She was right about my getting lost. I was fine on the M4, and quite efficient, with the help of the gizmos, at finding the correct roundabout near Bracknell, but the mobile home park was a sweet fairy-tale confection, a bit like the Gugelhupfs, and I was soon circling the park with my mobile phone to my ear. 'Go west, young man,' she said, 'and you'll find me next to a nice garden and blue trash can.' Most of the gardens looked the same, and the general ambience was of somewhere at the end of nowhere, a place that closed the rest of the world out with white fencing from the DIY store. Residents had made what seemed like competitive little grottoes of plaster gnomes and woodland creatures, and some were fairy dells, but I ignored them and the barking of dogs in my search for Carolyn. Where was Denver in all of this, or the wide open road to Mexico, or the woman, hip to the souls of sensitive men, who was played on-screen by Sissy Spacek and later by Kirsten Dunst?

'You made it,' she said. She stood at the door in a dressing gown and her face was shaded by the conifer trees above her cabin. Inside, she had packed a lot of the stuff I remembered from her old flat in Belsize Park. On the table, there were trinkets from Sausalito and a bowl of turquoise from Santa Fe. She told me the mobile home had seemed the best option after a life of different houses and flats. She was interested in the properties of my car's GPS and whether it could be relied on. 'Well, we had maps,' she said, 'but they didn't use them. The boys didn't know where they were going. Not really. They just knew that they wanted to go.' She was in dispute with historians of her own life, and she wasn't feeling well, but she took up her More cigarettes and her Zippo and fancied herself free for an afternoon of reminiscing and setting the record straight. She was upset, she said, by female memoirists and novelists who made out she was some sort of drudge, or somehow a 'deficient keeper of the flame'. It disturbed her that so much of the criticism came from women who wanted to claim a greater closeness to the men, and who went about it, oftentimes, by denigrating the wives. She told me she'd put up with it for years. 'They don't know what it was like, most of them, these squeezes or passing heroines.' We went to her dining table and she had a few bites of the bagel and a corner of a cake. 'I'm not much of an eater,' she said, 'but I used to love preparing food for the kids and whoever came by.'

Carolyn was amazed by the fame surrounding that part of her life, the interest in Kerouac and her husband and their trips. She said it was a stressful time for her, being young, far from the Zen fantasy that later fuelled the hopes of a billion backpackers, and she told me it was all part of the great big fiction that engulfed her. She'd told her own story in a book, *Off the Road*, about the trials of being a beat woman, and not beat enough, with diapers to wash and a home to keep going.

She liked discussing books. She'd read one of mine and wanted to talk about holy fools. She wanted then to talk about secondary characters, the people in fiction who illuminate the main people by sidelight, and who are themselves often overlooked along the way. At one point I took out my phone. 'They always want pictures,' she said, and when I asked who 'they' were, she said, 'the fans'. She pushed the clasps in her hair and said it was hard to look nice when you were eighty-nine.

The bed was covered with an Indian bedspread. A cold light was passing through the blinds and she sat on the edge, fixing a spool onto an old reel-to-reel recorder that was plugged in beneath her bookshelves. When she pressed play, there were a few crackles and then the voices of drunk men talking on a home-made recording. She told me it was made in her house in San Jose during one long night of excess in 1952. Kerouac and her husband were reading from *Remembrance of Things Past*, imitating Proust, imitating great actors, and then Kerouac's voice began to sing 'A Foggy Day in London Town'. He didn't know the words but he knew the feeling and gave it all he had.

'They were just boys,' she said. 'Just boys. But they had seen the sun together and that is everything.'

And just like that, Carolyn slipped away again. Her emails would still arrive and we made another date for lunch but she wasn't well enough when the day came. She found the summer very trying, and, thankfully, her son John came from America, and was with her when she died that September. I didn't even know about it, having disappeared again into that world where you don't see the people you want to see. I've never crossed her name out of the old address book, and I wake sometimes and imagine it must be time to drive out west and see Carolyn under the conifer trees. ■

Jay G. Ying

Scheherazade Conjoining (31)

☰

They said: There is the eye of the citizens · bystander · belligerent ·
blameless · blamed whose history has colonized the captured · in the
distance created by time · and there is the eye of the · actual photographer
(Gina Apostol)

☰

Every channel is *News at Eight* repeating infinitely. Another insolvent
country declares their intentions to be closer to the stars. A satellite
is launched. Annexation begins indefinitely. Breaking: every body
avoids katabasis if they can help it because descension is the inversion
of flight. The invader's military retreat from their occupied zones is
one inevitability. One missile obliterates the nameless farmers off
the international stage almost instantly. Still, Typhoon Amaterasu
begins to sink not soon enough over what is left of Indonesia. On the
right the sun is setting across the Matterhorn and the sky is inflamed,
is incredible. And below, those indigenous islands still are smoking
whenever the dinner trolley passes down intimately. Inanna is an
answer to a question on mortality they spot on the seat in front. They
have made so many trips from the interior of a country down towards
their coasts, and it is just all so intuitive. Thirst, the promise of water,
leads to life eventually. So they switch it all off; plead for a refill.
Ignore it. Inconsequential. Insubstantial. Incomprehensible. Yet in

that dark reflection on their screen, their necklace smuggled with lapis lazuli glows like an ingot, incites a rash on their neck, invites another story into this costly domain.

☰

'One offal omen

when I witness a nymph semi-living splutter up against the Saran Wrap of my in-flight exotic fruit salad repeatedly

How many emperors might crumble in the time to drive my head through this reinforced windowpane I lean on

Like that moribund fly I guzzle up the condensation of the aluminium cover to taste the uncanny peeled sweat of the machine

Main sacrifice:
two tasteless balls of lumpen white meat in an ethnic sauce the shade of terracotta to which I add enough salt to kill then preserve a body

What poor beasts were these lumps cut out from: two scoops of the liver the hips the ovaries the eyes

A bad dream

I could fall in love with this necrotravel and its everlasting flight

The comfort-class company of the riverboat ferry turned cargo turned warship, the locomotive train, the spitfire and the drone

Is it a surprise then that I survive like this, wearing bodies like scalding hand towels

There is a small kick to think I can reminisce the sound of date pits falling onto gold platters still

weekend getaways to guess where the palm trees once gossiped in the Hanging Gardens of Babylon

back in the days of my empire, timeshares in China, watch two imported white tigers forced to mate, male slaves in our garden playing the harp

testosterone in the vines mixed with the scent of blood, Springtime, eyes closed

necks out, spice in the breeze, executions in the sunlight, tang of death from the rotting flesh or fruit perfume

just another eternal day in his kingdom

No! All that was ancient history? Here is the divine booming interruption of a bulletin. Our pilot invites in the turbulence: abnormal storms seize the white skin over our metal exterior

while to my right that child squirms in his seat like a quarry in its
cage, eyes as wide as dessert spoons
as sunken as two lakes on a mountain

So lucky you were not born a girl, back in my day

Eight minutes later the call for a doctor spurts out and the pale cabin
crew materialise among us in an instant

like spirits of the dead

We think we can see the patient four rows in front
one large male shape half contorted half transmuting into a mass-
produced figurine

migrating earth with either too much or too little brown sugar

his meek groans in the face of death escape his small pursed lips like
a whistle

a slither of steam leaves the ground

a soul lost at the moment when an American turns around to ask

Do you think he has brought something contagious back
from his homeland?

But really all the minor will witness is a stranger jab a pen into that man's sponge

flesh which seems to pull all surrounding sound inwards
flesh that bubbles like a secret stale soufflé
flesh like the hushed opening of a bomb, and for a second, I expected something terrible

as if I was still narrating in a long age of monsters and flashy heroes

After modernity I am quick to learn that everything continues with no epic nor lesser consequence

There was: the white noise after the disturbance only, as a blanket is pulled over that man who could be dead or just sleeping only, his overhead light turned off only, right leg locked towards the aisle outwards only

like a hitch-hiker hailing down another realm

I saw that sock spitefully picked out by his wife two sizes too small tighten its leisure grip on one drumstick leg and leave its puffy gnaw of polyester teeth behind

grey limb swollen like a kink in a grey river

Our pilot did not lie
we soon shook in that space like slack atoms

Something large and classical activated inside me

Every potential flay of lightning
linked to a memory of broiled skin breaking out once struck
a punishment for the foreign insurgents I witnessed many times at
the side of my King in my first Arabian life

When the body of our plane's shadow overwhelmed the body of the lake
on the screen

I dreamt of a giant man, a leviathan
tearing into this steamed vehicle's roof as if it were the bulging lid of
a ready meal in the microwave

How disappointing

only to find a line of ants inside calmly crawling on the carpet towards
those exit doors that in the dark, that in the smoke, grows like a portal
like a black TV box
like a mouth
like a hole that will never be closed

Thank any God, our emergency is celestially authorised

And we begin our slow volatile descent over a mountain range
somewhere between two colossal, two cruel continents'

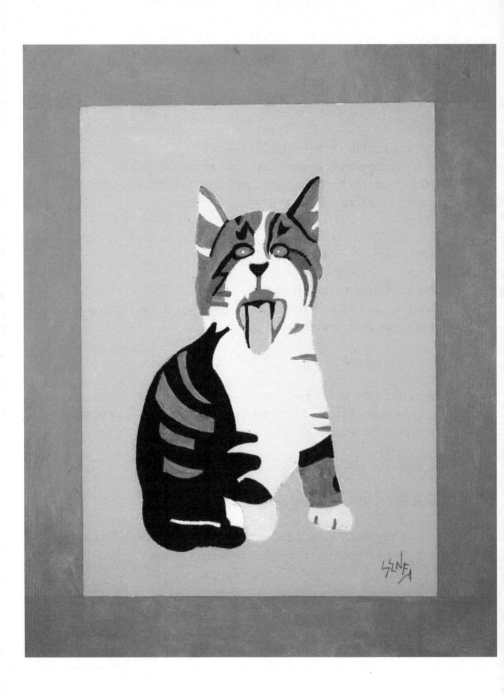

Cat, 2016
Fountain House Gallery

HOW TO COUNT LIKE A PRO

Amy Leach

Good morning, Animals, and welcome to our first lecture. Can we offer you some puddles to drink? Please settle down, quit flapping, stop bellowing, retract your claws and lower your tails; thank you. Now, before we start edifying you, we're going to level with you. We've been concerned about your performance lately, which has been, well, less than enterprising. You just don't seem very plugged-in. Of course we understand that you are all anachronisms and that as anachronisms you have been 'grandfathered in'. We are not expecting you to become astroanimals or anything; but out of concern for your viability, we'd like to help you salvage your sagging careers and regain some relevance. This is an opportunity to hitch your wagon to a star! Humans are stars, having risen through the echelons of Earth to practically transcend it! If you attend our lectures we will not microwave all of you and we can help you get on the same page as us.

We used to be on different pages ourselves, or sometimes not even on a page at all. Our old calendar had only ten pages – ten months, starting with March and ending in December, which left winter just a numberless stretch of days. Since we reformed the calendar, adding January and February, there are no longer any off-calendar days. All days are on-calendar. The calendar reformation is a good example of what is possible – you can reinvent calendars, you can even reinvent yourselves. We hear different ones of you going around saying 'It is my lot to be a yak' or 'It is my lot to be a mudpuppy' or 'It is my lot to be a green water dragon' or 'It is my lot to be a bagworm' or 'It is my lot to be a megabat'. Do you not realize how fatalistic you sound? You sound like turnips! In this series of lectures, we are going to set out some important principles to help you break out of 'turnip thinking'.

To begin, let's discuss the power of numbers. As the father of eugenics wrote, 'Whenever you can, count.' Larry here will now hand out stickers with this motto on them, for you to post on your burrows and bowers, the sides of your nests, the entrances to your caves. The counting habit is going to help you cultivate the three Rs – rationality, reasonableness and regulation – you with your unregulated ids – and eliminate subjectivity. Subjectivity is like a banshee, nonexistent and therefore easy to eliminate. Sometimes, when you see the emerald and ruby and sapphire sparkles on the snow, it seems like you are rich; sometimes it seems you can't get along without someone, seems the winter will never end, seems the moon is abnormally big coming over the mountains. But measurement dispenses with all the seeming: the bank account is low, the moon is normal-sized, etc.

Count whenever you can! We use our fingers and toes, but you can use your toes and toes, or pincers or flippers or whatever, and you snakes can make toothmarks in a branch. However you do it, you should start counting everything you see – clods, azaleas, skunks. Plants being stationary are generally easier to count than animals, though stay away from furze because it has no plural. 'Furze' is one of those uncountable nouns like 'information' or 'butter'. When you do start counting animals, start by counting strangers – and remember not to look in their eyes, lest they lose countability. Counting strangers is like counting words in a foreign language. If someone writes to us in Kickapoo – 'Ämănutei wīpani' or 'Măgānăguhanu, nezegwize, ăhitci īna Wīza'kä'ą' – counting the words comes easy. But if somebody writes to us in English – 'I need you' or 'I don't need you' or 'Let's get revenge on the old buzzard' – we can get caught up in the meaning and forget to count. Meaning undermines objectivity.

The words that really matter are the words for numbers – one, two, three, four, five – or yan, tan, tether, mether, pip – or hant, tant, tothery, forthery, fant – but see there, how arbitrary words are! Someday we should replace all our words with numerals. Numerals are absolute, and think of their stamina compared with words. Numerals never run out – you just add one more, one more, one more: sheep four, sheep five, sheep six. You don't have to come up with a new name for every sheep, just a new sheep for every number, and if sheep seven gets squished, another one can take her place. Names aren't as transposable, and names can sound like children's songs, like the village of Nobbin and the hill of Nabbingo. Names are also unnecessarily meaningful, like the old Armenian words for the days of the month. They had a day called Tumultuous and one called Hermit and one called Dispersion, and a day called Beginning, which came right before the day called Beginningless. How today could be Beginningless when yesterday was Beginning is a boggling question dispelled by calling the days Sixteen and Seventeen.

Now, we humans have the advantage that our modern culture is principally composed of countable things. Sports and politics and business and social media, with their rankings and followers and prices and indexes and polls and points, help us keep our heads thoroughly in the numbers – unlike you giraffes with your heads in the clouds. We do our best to quantify the clouds, but they and other components of the weather elude us sometimes. Lightning is elusive, incendiary, highfalutin. (Literature used to be like lightning, but now that we have subjected it to Big Data, literature is more like sheep. Never have we burst into flames when we got hit by a sheep.)

Anyhow, if ever we get flummoxed by the weather, we can always turn to our clocks. Clocks are the consummate counters, even better than bankers because they never sleep and especially they never dream. No minute is off-clock. What we know about ourselves, from research articles we've read, is that what we find most attractive in a face is symmetry. It was inevitable, then, that we would fall so hard for clocks. We have actually entered into an exclusive relationship with them and can't imagine being tempted by someone less symmetrical.

To be a great counter, like a clock, one must be on guard against perceiving distinction – but of course where there are no distinctions, none shall be perceived. You animals have your own advantage in that within your species you all have the same faces, like nickels, so you probably don't even need to worry about sticking to strangers when you count! Your relatives look just like your strangers, and it's not like you hamsters would be counting hamsters without a hitch but then your dream hamster scurries by, making you lose count. This unfortunately does happen to us sometimes, though not with dream hamsters. The worst is when we've been counting people with clocklike consistency but then the granddaughters run by. Granddaughters mess up the metric, and they grapple us to them with their little fingers. This is called the adoration problem and it contaminates the purity of calculation.

The point is to never be snagged by the particular. 'Everybody to count for one, nobody for more than one,' wrote Jeremy Bentham, and this means that everybody is everybody. Everybody says, 'I'm not everybody,' but of course everybody is. Just listen to two everybodies arguing about who is everybodier: it is as ridiculous as two twenties arguing over who is twentier.

We feel sorry for those in the adoration business, the adorazzi, the mystics and musicians, muddleheads when it comes to numbers. 'Better is one day in your courts than a thousand elsewhere' – the Psalmist's singling out of one day like that is so delusional: there are no deluxe days, just as there are no deluxe hamsters. Every day is every day; every day is precisely the same little square inch as every other day. The Psalms are full of bad math and seemings and vicissitudes. There is nothing like a musical instrument for exacerbating vicissitudes, and in the Psalms you find lyred people, luted people, fluted people, tamborined people, completely abandoned to their vicissitudes, and hare-brained harpist kings longing for someone invisible. (Bad enough to crush on someone visible.) We think of the Psalms – actually the whole Bible – with dismay. Here we are computing on our computers, and there is Miriam getting all carried away on the timbrel. 'Still playing the timbrel, Miriam?' – that question really encapsulates our thoughts about old testaments.

The one distinction that is really valuable to make is between Essential and Superfluous. Up to a certain number things are Essential, and over that they are Superfluous. As names go, Superfluous is actually a good one to have on hand. Any offspring beyond two or three you can name Superfluous. Having counted ninety-nine of his sheep into the fold, the sensible shepherd will call the hundredth one Superfluous and turn in for the night. No need to traipse around in the chilly, rainy, brambly dark, searching for a lamb called Superfluous. Counting enables one to distinguish between Sufficient and Surplus, although somehow in India the cows got into the sacred racket, which makes no such distinction. (Indian math has a history of being irrational – India is where they came up with irrational numbers and mathematical infinity.)

When we were two we loved all the cows, and every hamster was our dream hamster. But then we grew into good calculators. Calculation converts the sacredest things into inventory. To milk the milkable, beef the beefable, boot the bootable – to utilize everything we can, offal, tripe, excrement. Not all wines turn out wonderfully but you can still serve the inferior ones after the guests are plastered. Though live koalas are a bit fragile, koala pelts are 'able to withstand hard usage'. In our next lecture, this Thursday, entitled 'How to Stay Relevant in the Modern World', we will elaborate on this exciting principle, so please be sure to bring all your little branchmates, cavemates, warrenmates and puddlemates. ■

A PORTRAIT OF MY MOTHER

Michael Collins

The first time my mother suffered a stroke, she kept it a secret. One minute she was driving home and then suddenly everything became blurry and her Renault 5 was bumping along the verge. She did not go to her doctor because she knew he would take away her driving licence. In hindsight, that was the year when my mother announced that she was going to move back to Cheshire. She was in her mid-seventies and her cottage in the Cotswolds was at the bottom of a steep hill, which she told us she found increasingly difficult to manage on foot during the winter months. My mother was from Cheshire; her sister-in-law and my brother lived up there, so she thought it would be a good idea to move near them. Our father had died some fifteen years earlier, and she had been on her own ever since. She was healthy and active, if a little bored; looking for a new home would keep her occupied. Uncharacteristically, she bought a town house with a patio but no garden, although she promptly planted roses under the conservatory window and trained a clematis along the wall. The house was just across the river from the medieval town centre, and she would walk over the bridge most mornings to buy the paper and do her shopping.

A few years later, she had a massive stroke. That day I happened to be nearby, but by the time I arrived, the doctor had been and gone.

My mother was sitting in an armchair in her dressing gown, looking flustered and embarrassed, but strangely triumphant. Her face was white and swollen, and although the left side was drooping a little, she could speak clearly. The next morning I telephoned the doctor and was told to bring her in to the surgery. She could barely stand, let alone walk, and for all her outward display had no strength. I went over to the surgery and insisted that a doctor visit her at home, and later that morning a different doctor came, one who seemed much more sympathetic than her regular GP. She introduced herself, sat down and gently asked a few questions before taking my mother's pulse and listening to her breath. On her way out, the doctor gave me some advice which was lost on me at the time: plan for the long term, she said.

We sold the Renault and bought a reconditioned stairlift. She made light of it, but the stairlift was the first thing you saw when you came through the front door. She would sit on its folding plastic chair, stoically keeping the button pressed as it pulled her along at one mile an hour. On the advice of an occupational therapist who had gone around the house making suggestions about grip rails and trip hazards, we took away all the rugs, had a builder construct a concrete ramp outside the back door and mounted a key safe on the wall so that health workers could gain access. I would take her out in the car, her walking frame in the boot, but she became essentially housebound. We arranged for care workers to visit three times a day. Most of them were kind, though constrained by time, and a couple were truly wonderful. One had a booming voice ('my boyfriend says I don't need a mobile phone') and you knew, when she arrived, that everything would be all right. Another, who mainly came in the evening, had something special about her that can only be described as goodness. Some of the other carers were a bit brusque, and my mother told me that one had bullied her. That person never came near the house again.

With the ramp and key safe and stairlift and the visits from the carers and doctors, my mother's home felt increasingly impersonal. She tried to put on a brave face but was miserable, and resented losing the ability to go out on her own. We had bought her an alarm button, which she was meant to wear as a necklace, but she refused, insisting that the rubber cord gave her a rash. One day I rang and the phone was off the hook. I phoned her neighbour, but she was out, as was my brother, so I drove from London only to find her watching television. She argued with the doctors about her medication, some of which she did not like and thought was unnecessary and threw away, and they became increasingly frustrated, not knowing exactly what medication my mother had taken. Meanwhile her blood pressure soared.

Late one afternoon my brother rang to tell me that the carers had discovered she had fainted, possibly due to a minor stroke or a TIA. He said that a doctor had been and that she was okay. My brother lived twenty minutes from her, so I urged him to go and see how she was, which he reluctantly agreed to do. An hour later, annoyed, he told me that she was fine. Three and a half hours later I arrived from London to find her in bed, grey-faced and exhausted. She slept most of the next day but by evening seemed on the mend, and I felt able to drive home when the last carer had settled her in for the night.

Inevitably, as the doctor kept warning her, a succession of minor strokes culminated in a devastating one. My aunt found her lying on the kitchen floor, and she was rushed to hospital. We had no idea how long she had lain there. Her face was so swollen that her features were altered, and her left arm was temporarily paralysed. For several days, she slept constantly and could not talk. When she tried, there was a long pause and then a sigh before she gave up. The hospital was a sprawling, two-storey complex built in the 1970s in the middle of nowhere and had a tall metal incinerator chimney that was visible for miles. The stroke unit was superb – new equipment, well staffed, a positive aura about it – whereas the geriatric ward, where she was placed, was like lost property. Patients languished on their own, waiting for waiting's sake. There were hardly any staff and the prevailing mood was despondency. As soon as she had her wits back, all she wanted to do was go home. She looked wretched lying there in her hospital gown; everyone on the ward looked wretched. One evening I arrived just as dinner had been cleared. Opposite my mother was an extremely old woman, a bush of stark white hair drawn back over her skeletal head. She was staring at a juicy orange in front of her on a plate. Her arthritic hands were like claws – it must have been at least a decade since she was able to peel an orange. A nurse came by, pushing a trolley, and when I asked her to please help the woman eat her orange, the nurse informed me that she was busy dispensing medicines, and then caught herself. 'I'm so sorry,' she said. 'This job makes you tunnel-visioned.' As the nurse fed her a segment at a time, the old woman sucked the fruit with her eyes closed, the look on her face beatific.

Without consulting my brother and sister, I researched local residential homes and made appointments to visit them. One was run-down and far from public transport links, which would present a problem for my sister, who does not drive. Another was starkly institutional, with painted breeze-block walls, sharp neon lighting and a view as bare as its walls. The third had a welcoming atmosphere but was clearly underfunded and run by a hard-pressed local authority. The last one was reassuringly posh. Part of a new, exclusive housing development, the main building looked like the other large detached houses on the road, only bigger. There were warden-assisted flats with brick-paved courtyards, flower beds and hanging baskets, and a quasi-Alpine brick-and-timber building set around a bowling green. Ludicrously, there was even a Union Jack. The home was obviously expensive, but I was convinced that my mother had only a matter of months to live, a year at the very most. It was so much more comfortable than the other places, more like a Saga hotel than a residential home, that I felt sure she would like the idea of moving here. They told me that they had a guest room, which was mainly used for short-term respite, although sometimes people might come there for a week to see what it was like. When I showed my mother and brother and sister the brochure, they looked aghast, but eventually it was agreed that we would take her there to have a look the following weekend. As we were being shown around, my brother lagged behind, tight-lipped, but my mother admired the surroundings and found the culture reassuring. Afterwards, as we sat in the lobby drinking tea and eating small packets of biscuits, my mother decided that she would try it for a week.

A few days later we took her there with her little suitcase, which my sister helped her unpack, and together they placed a few pictures on the windowsill while we all made encouraging conversation. Before we left, my sister made a fuss of her and rubbed cream into her stiff hands. We were staying at my mother's house, which was only a twenty-minute walk away, and we would be back the next day, but we all knew that this marked a rupture in our family life and that things would never be the same.

My mother was born in a small Cheshire village in 1924. Her father, Ernest, had fought and been wounded at the Somme and he kept the bullet in a cigarette tin, which I would pester him to show me. According to my mother, his wartime experience had left him with a deep-rooted distrust of the French. Ernest worked as a travelling salesman for a stationery company and during the Depression twice had to take a cut in pay. I have no memory of any conversations with him and cannot recall the sound of his voice: he died when I was about eight years old. Ernest's father had been a refrigeration engineer at London's Smithfield meat market and was apparently very bright, but was an alcoholic. My mother told us that Ernest would search for him in the pubs on Friday nights to stop him spending his week's wages on booze. Florence, her mother, died a few years before Ernest and one of the only memories I have of her is visiting her in hospital and being taken up to the ward in an old-fashioned, caged metal lift. My mother always said how kind she was and in photographs she has a benign, round face. Towards the end of his life, Ernest moved into a residential home with a huge cedar tree in the garden. I remember my mother replacing the buttons on his trousers with zips. She once told us a story, which I liked her to retell, of how one day, walking home from school, Ernest passed her in the car but would not stop because she looked scruffy, which seemed so unlike my mother; she hated her school hat and was not wearing it that afternoon. In one of her albums, there is a photograph of her and her younger sister by the front door of their house, both sitting on a little tricycle. My mother sits behind, holding her sister as she stretches for the handlebars. Her sister is chubby-faced, while my mother already has her dark looks and finer features. In another picture, taken in almost the same place, they are teenagers, standing together in summer dresses. Her sister is looking at the camera straightforwardly, while my mother, sure of her good looks, holds her face at a slight angle.

In the early stages of the Second World War, my mother was working as a secretary in Manchester when a local reporter, writing a piece about how women would respond to the war, asked her what she intended to do. 'I'm not going to work in a factory!' she declared, presenting the perfect quote and photo opportunity. Her father warned her that she was now doomed to do just that, so she decided to enlist with the forces and volunteered to join the Wrens, because she liked their uniform the best. She served throughout the war and in 1946 sailed on HMS *Formidable* to Trincomalee, in what was then Ceylon.

She met my father at a dance in Stockport just after the war. He had dark features too. They were a striking couple and in the photos of their early married life they look glamorous in the folds of their forties clothes. But while she had a confident way of facing a camera, he looked slightly ill at ease. I can remember a picture of them standing beside their car on the road above Lake Windermere, my father in his dark overcoat and trilby, my mother in a hat and coat and pale scarf, looking like they are in a film, but when I search their albums, each is pictured on their own with the car. I wonder how it was for them back then, driving around the Lakes, taking each other's picture by the side of the road. In the photo of my mother, my father's shadow shows the stark outline of his hat, hand and camera. Some years ago, looking through old postcards in a junk shop, I found a sepia-printed reproduction of a tiny figure silhouetted in a landscape, sitting on a low wall and looking out over a bay. Although the solitary, middle-aged man is too small for his features to be visible, I know the look on his face, and I know that silence as his face stares off into the distance.

My father was born in Manchester in 1922. When he and his sister were quite young, the family moved to Liverpool, where his mother's family lived. Harry, his father, died before I was born, and May, his mother, when I was still very young. Family lore was that Harry lost everything in the Wall Street Crash and May's family bailed him out. There are only a few photographs of Harry: in one, he is walking along a boardwalk in a well-cut woollen suit, his hands clasped behind him. His face was slightly rounder than my father's and he had an air of assurance. The only time I remember my father talking about him was when he quoted one of Harry's ditties: *Cheshire lad born and bred, strong in arm, thick in head.* The voice my father used when relaying this was utterly alien from his own middle-class, Home Counties cadence. It was as though a tightly held secret had escaped his lips and we avoided eye contact.

The morning after my mother's first night at the residential home, I went to visit her and when I arrived I found her dressed and looking perky, as though she was on holiday. I had brought her a takeaway cappuccino from a cafe, and after she had drunk it, her face became flushed and she was raring to go. But there was nowhere to go and we did not know what to do. Lunch was hours away and I was even more reluctant to go into the lounge than she was, so we sat there in her room, trying to find something positive to talk about while we waited for my sister. Sitting in a room together, we were never able to have long conversations. Like bad tennis players, we could only exchange a few sentences before hitting the net and we were much better off talking while out doing something, our sparse dialogue serving as an aside. Over the next few days, my sister and I took it in turns visiting, eating overboiled vegetables in the dining room and sitting out in the garden alongside some of the other residents. After the third day, my mother told me that she would like to stay. It was only after she said 'I feel safe' that I realised how vulnerable she must have been at home.

My mother was eighty-two when she moved into the home, making her one of the youngest residents. She was still in relatively good shape. Apart from a slight paralysis in her left arm, she had recovered fully from the last stroke. Her memory seemed unaffected and she had all her wits about her. She could move around quite easily with the walking frame, so much so that my brother said that she was taking the frame for a walk. Her window looked out onto the garden, which faced west, and come dusk she would absorb herself in the sunsets, which were often spectacular in that part of Cheshire. There was a magnificent oak tree in the middle of the lawn, and we would sit watching a pair of crows who patrolled their space. One had a white feather on its wing and would strut around, coming quite close to the window. My mother would shoo it away, which made no sense to me, and I would speak up on the crow's behalf and my mother would look at me quizzically and say: 'Do you dear?'

On her windowsill, she had arranged a pair of mahogany bookends that my parents had brought back from Ghana before we were born, and some framed family pictures, including one of my father taken in California about forty years ago. In it he is standing beside some rocks in a summer shirt and shorts, holding a smile as he squints a little in the sunshine. The photograph has become quite bleached out, and his shirt is the same colour as the rocks, but his head is as clear as ever, although you have to look into the shadows under his eyes to see his features. The sky has deteriorated into an unworldly hue, in contrast to the unquestionable then-and-there of my father's presence, which gives the picture the vivid but mythical air of a dream. Sometimes, when she was feeling especially gloomy, my mother would say how much she missed him. 'I just want to be with your father again,' she would say, and I would feel awkward and look away.

All of the staff were locals and there was something reassuring about their soft Cheshire voices. Most of the time the residents' doors were kept open so that the staff could look in as they passed by, checking everyone was all right. You would hear them talking or calling out as they made their way along the corridor. To some of them it was a job, which they conducted with varying degrees of commitment and professionalism; to others, it was more of a vocation. The older ones, in particular, were both wise and kind. They knew how to help my mother wash and dress in a gentle way; they remembered what she did and did not like to eat; they could judge when to jolly her along and when not to; when to stay and chat and when to leave her alone. The truth is, they saw much more of our mother than we did and they had a better understanding of how she was coping. When things did go wrong, or when we needed to raise an issue with the home, we knew that even if we had cause to make a complaint, we were reliant on their goodwill. I was grateful to them for looking after my mother, but as subtly as I could, I let them know that I was keeping a hawk-eye on her. There were a few carers who regularly looked after my mother, and with whom she became friends. My wariness wore off with them, but not with the manager, who I regarded as representing the interests of the private health corporation. One day when I was visiting, a couple of months after my mother's arrival, I found that the only spare parking place out front was the one reserved for the manager. Making sure no one could see me from the window, I deliberately ran over the little wooden sign as I parked in her space.

Most of the other residents' families seemed to be very wealthy, which added to my sense of estrangement. Maybe because I was struggling financially, I could never quite shake off the feeling that we had come in through the back door. It was an upholstered world where I did not belong, and the only newspaper I ever saw, including in my mother's room, was the *Daily Mail*. Given my mother's rapid decline, the cost was almost irrelevant. In the twelve months before she entered the home she had aged years, and had gone from being an independent elderly woman to an invalid. I could not see her lasting another six and, for the foreseeable future, she could easily afford the cost of the home.

Gradually, my mother settled in, but for all the efforts of the staff, she did not socialise much. She would eat lunch with three other residents because the carers had assigned the four of them a table together, but that was the extent of her social routine. My brother, who lived close by, visited her like clockwork every Tuesday. He would phone her beforehand, collect some shopping and supermarket flowers, and stay for half an hour. Very occasionally, they would go to the quiz morning, but apart from lunch, most days she stayed in her room which, with some of her pictures that we had brought from her house, looked like a small, temporary home away from home.

My mother always loved animals, and they seemed to bond with her. I can remember once seeing her in the garden with her Siamese cat, picking him up and holding his face close to a rose so that he could smell its scent. Now and then, animals were brought to the home to visit the residents. There was a dog who came most weekends and for a while – until some of the residents complained that it was unhygienic – they adopted a small black-and-white female cat called Phoenix. One evening when we were talking on the phone, my mother mentioned a donkey the height of her television. I was probably not listening properly and asked her to explain what she meant. A little annoyed, she told me that a donkey had visited the home that afternoon and had come into her room, and sure enough, when I saw her the next weekend, the noticeboard in reception was full of snaps of the residents with an elderly brown donkey, which was the talk of the place. About a year later, I dropped by one weekday lunchtime to find a small horsebox parked out the front. The residents were lined up in their wheelchairs as the donkey was led slowly into the lounge, stopping to let them stroke his ears. For those too infirm or otherwise unable to come into the lounge, the donkey was taken to their rooms. My mother was waiting for him like a long-lost friend; I do not think I have ever seen her look so happy, and when she rummaged in her handbag to tip the handler, the donkey thought she had some treats and shoved his nose right in. I took a photograph of the two of them and she kept this on her mantelpiece. One day someone brought in some lizards. 'What were they like?' I asked her. She replied that they were charming.

My father was only sixty-three when he had the heart attack. On the evening of the attack, I had spoken to him, but rather than keeping the call short, for once he seemed to want to talk for longer. If I were ever able to undo just one thing from my past, I would have ignored my then girlfriend's insistence to get off the telephone because we were running late. When I returned home later that evening, there was a note on the door. He held on for three days, never regaining consciousness. On the last day, knowing he was dying, my mother asked me whether I would like to take my father's hand for the last time, but I just could not touch him. His face was purple-red and he did not look like my dad any more. We had never been tactile, let alone expressive about how we felt, and now that it really mattered, it was too late.

A few months after the funeral, while my mother was sorting through papers for my father's probate, she realised that she could not find his birth certificate and wrote to the Home Office for a copy. A reply came stating that they had no such record. The only place where she had not looked was an old Second World War metal case, which my father had kept padlocked in the loft. Inside, she found a birth certificate in the name of Cohen. She telephoned his sister to ask her about this and the story emerged: Harry was Jewish, whereas May was from a prominent Catholic family. My father and his sister were raised as Catholics and had their names changed to Collins when they were young. My mother told us that shortly before her wedding, my father had written to her to say that there was a family secret that he would divulge if she asked him to, but if she did not, he would consider the matter closed. She never asked him. Her reasoning was that if he had wanted to tell her, he would have done. According to my sister, a few days before he died, my father had received a telephone call from a long-lost cousin, who had come across him by chance. My mother made light of it, treating this disclosure as an entertaining anecdote. My sister, who had had a difficult relationship with our father, avoided discussing it with me, and my brother never mentioned it.

Not long afterwards, I can remember walking home late on a cold winter's night through Whitechapel and Spitalfields. I was wearing a thick Crombie overcoat, its collar turned up for warmth. It reminded me of a coat my father wore when I was a child. When he came home from work you would hear his shoes on the door scraper and you could feel the night air in the warm hallway. He travelled a lot and when he was home, he was busy. I was his favourite and the older I get, the more like him I look. Possibly I am reimagining the past to make sense of what I know now, but I wonder whether I ever had any intuition about there being something missing in his life – something he held back. He could be spontaneous and great fun, but ultimately he was slightly reserved. I realise now that actually he was hidden, and this was killing him. Coming along Brick Lane that night, the vestiges of Jewish London took on a whole new resonance, but it was alienating too, and I felt more of an outsider than ever before, and afraid of not belonging anywhere, a fear I realised I had felt all my life, and still do.

Some years later, supposedly out of the blue, my aunt called to tell me that she had stumbled across an address for Ronald, her long-lost cousin. His name was Collins too. I took down the details and wrote him a letter which began: I am the younger son of Basil Leon Collins. Ronald wrote back via return of post, surprised but pleased to hear from me, and told me that his father, Sidney (Harry's brother), was still alive, and asked if we would like to meet. We arranged that I would drive to Hale with my aunt. The houses became grander and the drives longer until eventually we reached their address and there was a Rolls-Royce parked outside, which made us both groan. Ronald and his wife, Carrie, came out to greet us. Ronald looked as though he could have been my father's brother: he had exactly the same comb-over, wore the same check shirt, cravat and cardigan, and even the same heavy leather shoes. I found this very disconcerting. On the doorstep, he stopped me and asked why, after all these years, I had got in touch? But Carrie brushed his question aside and led me into the living room. It was opulent and at the far end, sitting side by side in a couple of deep armchairs, their round faces filled with tears, were Sidney and his wife, Dollie. Even though it was a completely different house to any I had known, and even though I felt uncomfortable around Ronald, for the first time in my life I felt like I was home. Sidney was reaching forward, holding out his hands towards me and he said: 'Welcome, I know why you're here,' and Dollie gave me a big, wet kiss and a handwritten family tree.

For the first few years there was one crisis after another and I would visit at least every other weekend from London, staying in the room at the top of my mother's house. It had a skylight, as opposed to a window, so that although you could leave it open and hear the birdsong, you had no idea where you were. Apart from my aunt (with whom I had a strained relationship), I did not know anyone else in the town, and the only things I could find to do were to swim in the local brine pool, which was only open in summer, or go to a pub to watch football.

During this period I began working on an art commission in the next county and this enabled me to stay in my mother's house for a few days at a time. She clung on to the fact that although she now lived in a residential home, she still maintained a house in the town. I would bring her the post, which she would studiously open, dealing swiftly with utility bills and other domestic matters. Her greatest joy was going out, although she now had to use a wheelchair, and the only thing that prevented us from doing so was heavy rain. Her feet were so swollen that it was hard to keep her slippers on, and if you bumped her toes even slightly, she would wince. She could not keep her feet on the pedals in the wheelchair, so I made a footplate with a broken cheeseboard and attached this to the front with some shoelaces. Inside the home the central heating was always on high, so keeping her warm outside was a major challenge, not helped by her refusal to wear a headscarf or hat. She caved in on the blanket, but from the waist up insisted on looking her best. Her only outings were with me, which meant two weeks would go by between them, and she would often remark on how the flowers and shrubs along the path had changed with the weather and the season. Our route led past a long row of small Victorian houses with tiny front gardens and bay windows, and we came to know the moon-faced dog in one and the sleepy, elderly cat behind scratched net curtains in another. There was a mini-roundabout at the end of the road, with a zebra crossing, and cars would nearly always slow down in anticipation, letting us cross. If they did not, I would give them the filthiest of looks.

Once when we were going along, an SUV pulled up on the other side of the road and a man lowered the window, presumably wanting directions, before calling out that my mother had lost her slipper fifty yards back up the pavement. I thanked him, put the brake on and turned to walk back to fetch it. As I neared the slipper, an off-duty nurse, walking towards me, bent down and picked it up, smiling sympathetically. I thanked her and headed back to my mother, but as I reached her, there was the SUV driver and his wife, leaning out of the window. 'We did a U-turn at the mini-roundabout, but the nurse got there first!' and waving, they drove off. I busied myself putting the slipper back on and hurried along, grateful that she could not see the tears in my eyes.

If it was warm and dry enough, we would find a bench outside the church, get a couple of takeaway coffees and watch people cross the square. My mother would look so intently, she could have been on holiday in Rome. I would buy a slice of cake and break off bite-sized pieces which she would examine between her arthritic fingers, like a jeweller. If it was raining or too cold, we would go to our favourite cafe. With the cheeseboard mounted at the front, my mother's wheelchair took up quite a lot of space, and we would have to rearrange the chairs to make room, but the owner was always pleased to see us and never seemed to mind us leaving the table covered in crumbs. I would position my mother so that she could see the whole cafe, and she would sit with her thick coat unzipped and peeled over her shoulders, staring at the other customers with the unselfconsciousness of a child.

Whenever possible, we would go back to the house. There was an excellent fishmonger near the church and we would wheel up, so that she could choose something in the window. Roles reversed, she sat at the table looking at the newspaper while I cooked. She liked her daily glass of wine, and if she had the energy, we would go to the wine merchants and she would take her time choosing a bottle of red before shakily retrieving her bank card from her huge handbag and handing it over with a flourish. She had never really had much of a sweet tooth but we would often find half-eaten boxes of chocolates in her room, and I would buy her soft fruit gums in little paper bags, which we would eat as we went along. She would have liked me to have taken her to a supermarket because that was one of the things she missed most from ordinary life, but the memories of all those times trudging behind her in the aisles as a kid were ingrained too deeply for me to rise to this, and only at my most magnanimous was I able to take her to the mini Marks & Spencer, where the look of delight on her face filled me with shame.

Sometimes we would cross over the bridge and take the river path, and if she was in particularly fine form, we would go for miles, all the way through the woods to the playing fields, making a circuit of them. The tarmac paths were fairly smooth and we could go along at a brisk pace, her face flushed in the fresh air, no desire to turn back. She liked to go over the footbridge leading to the memorial for the American fighter pilot who crashed his burning plane there to avoid hitting the town, a history she repeated every time we passed it. Sometimes I got it wrong and she became tired and cold, and we would have to rush back, but when everything was going well, I used to ask her if she had had a good day, and she would say, in her slightly feeble voice, 'I've had a great day,' and she meant it.

I wanted to take her portrait and one afternoon I set up my camera on a tripod in the garden. She went along with it to humour me, and possibly because she liked the attention, but some of the other residents could see us and we both felt self-conscious. My mother was never that keen on me taking her portrait. I had done one about ten years earlier, when she had visited me on the coast. At first, she pulled poses, and it was only when I said 'Come on Mum, this is important to me' that she opened up. My mother was always rather evasive – we both were, and had become used to circling each other – but for those few seconds with my hand on the camera's button, she stopped circling and stood still. A little while after the botched portrait in the garden, I showed her a picture of her cat, who was now living with my sister in London, that I had taken on my phone, and suggested that I try making a portrait of her with it. Impressed by the one of the cat, she held her face up for me to photograph. This was not quite what I had in mind and, a few pouts later, I gave up. On my next visit, I brought an enlarged print that I had made of the cat's portrait. She held it carefully and traced her finger along his whiskers. When I asked her if she would like me to do hers, she said, 'Yes, let's,' and this time she took it more seriously, and when I showed the portrait to her on the phone's screen, she was as pleased as I was. After that, we would take her portrait nearly every time I visited her. Sometimes we would take two or three, if the first one did not look good, but rarely did I try more than a couple of times because then it turned into an ordeal. Taking the portrait became something we would do as part of our day together: it was something she gave me to take home; it was her way of telling me the things she did not say.

No matter how well the day went, I always had that sinking feeling wheeling her back into the home. We would arrive just in time for supper, when the carers were in the corridor with their trolleys. By early evening, the home would be quiet and the corridors deserted. I would say goodbye and stand outside her door, watching her before I walked off. There are only so many times you can say goodbye not knowing if this might be for the last time, and yet the next time it would be the same, as it would the time after that, and the time after that. However tiring it was driving home to London, I needed that space and privacy of being alone in the car after saying goodbye to her, pounding along in the outside lane.

Meanwhile, my mother's blood pressure remained alarmingly high and the doctor was convinced she was dumping some of the tablets and warned her that a stroke might likely paralyse her, leaving her unable to swallow rather than killing her. Eventually, after a series of arguments, he told her that she would be assigned an alternative doctor. I begged him to give her another chance, insisting that I could convince her to follow his instructions. He relented, but when I tried to reason with her, she was furious and with real venom in her voice accused me of bullying her.

The high blood pressure made her anger worse and she had taken to shouting at my brother. Every time she raged at me, I would tell her in the calmest voice possible that the way she was acting was not helping either of us, which infuriated her. She would grip the arms of her chair, jaw clamped, glowering at me, while I wondered whether I really was being a bully or just trying to be responsible, or both. I doubt she had any idea of quite how immature I felt passing off this role of a middle-aged man looking after his mother, or how it was dominating my life. Before her stroke, I would phone her once a week and see her every couple of months; but now I was calling her every day and driving back and forth several times a month. My sister and I tried to share responsibilities, but because she did not drive, I took the lion's share and in emergencies, it was me who made for the motorway. Once I went to New York for work, the longest and farthest I had been away since her devastating stroke, and when the plane landed back at Heathrow, my smartphone lit with a flood of urgent messages, and I went straight from the airport to my car to the hospital.

Over the course of the first few years, a pattern emerged. Things would go smoothly for a month or so and then my mother would have a TIA or a stroke. Sometimes she would be taken to the hospital, sometimes the home would simply call a doctor. Once she fell, breaking a hip, which was a catastrophe as it led to lengthy incarceration on the geriatric ward and her weight then dropped so much, she became too weak to return to the home. There was an old Chinese woman in the same ward and her relatives would arrive with home-made hot meals and pretend that they could not understand English when the nurses tried to prevent them from taking the food into her room. Some of the English patients and visitors would exchange knowing looks, but they were no fools; their mother recovered far quicker than the others. I ended up confronting the matron and showed her the photographs I had taken of the untouched, inappropriate meals. I also told her that I had photographed my mother's notes, a bluff that unnerved her. Sour-faced, she agreed to let me bring in food, the only condition being that it was in closed containers. I went back to my mother's house where I was staying and made chicken soup. For the next few days, I fed this to my mother by the spoonful and soon she recovered enough to go back to the home, where the carers could look after her properly.

Almost everyone I knew would phone me on my mobile number, but the residential home persisted in calling my landline, so on the rare times it rang, I would panic. I placed any long-term plans on hold and resigned myself to rearranging my immediate future so that I would be able to respond to my mother's needs at short notice. Not that I had a bulging diary or glittering social life, and my newly assumed guise as a caring son dealing with a dying mother excused all sorts of inadequacies. It also exacerbated them. I never used her disabled parking permit for myself, but I carried around a dying-mother visa.

Beneath her anger, my mother was becoming more and more depressed. She had now been living in the residential home for about three years and she had nothing to do. All her life, she had loved being in her garden, going for walks and reading outside. Getting some air was her remedy of choice and now she was trapped in a ruin of a body with nothing but daytime television. She had long since lost the ability to walk or even to stand for extended periods and she needed help to wash and get dressed. When we were little children, she used to say, 'When I get old just throw me under a bus,' which made no sense to us at that age. She now kept telling us that she just wanted it all to end. It was inconceivable that she would make one more Christmas, and as the next winter approached, and along with it the season when people of her age and condition would be most likely to die, I would be hoping for the news that I also dreaded. On top of this, the money was starting to run out. We maintained to the end that her pensions covered everything, but my brother, who was responsible for her financial affairs, had to start selling some of her investments, and we moved her into a smaller room on some pretext with the home's connivance.

My brother complained how hard it was for him to cope with her endlessly going on about wanting to die. He said that she would go on like this even to the deacon, who visited her every week. I was not sure how serious she was, but one Saturday I found her in utter despair, threatening to throw herself onto the ground, begging me to help her end it all. 'Please Michael,' she said, and I knew that, then and there, she really meant it. I had wondered if it would ever come to this, and had decided long ago that if she asked me three times, in a deliberate, conscious way, I would help her. I never stopped to wonder why she asked me, rather than my brother or sister; I suppose I took pride in the fact that she trusted me. Nor did I stop to consider that she was asking me to commit a crime for which I could be prosecuted for manslaughter. When I came back to see her the next morning, the first thing she said was that she really meant what she had told me, and she pleaded with me to assist her.

I knew I could not ask anyone for help, and did not tell my brother or sister. Later that week, I invited myself to a friend's house for tea. As well as being a doctor, she was a hypochondriac and kept a supply of strong painkillers and tranquillisers in her bathroom cabinet, which I raided without her knowledge. The next Saturday I carefully emptied the capsules into the cream of a chocolate eclair, my mother's favourite treat, placed it back inside the packet and drove up to Cheshire. I had decided that if she begged me a third time, emphatically, I would tell her that I had brought a special eclair for her, so that without saying it out loud, she would know it was poisoned. When I came into her room, she was slumped right over on one side in the chair. The strokes had severely damaged her spine and she could not sit upright for long. Often she would slide over to one side, having to be propped upright with cushions. The carers had arranged some for her, but she had slipped past these and looked very uncomfortable. There were no extra cushions to use, so I took a pillow from her bed and walked over to add it to the pile, but as I approached her with the pillow in my hands, her eyes widened in fright and I knew that she had changed her mind. She never mentioned suicide again and shortly afterwards asked the doctor to put her on antidepressants.

When my brother was nine, my parents sent him to boarding school. It was very exciting and I was envious of the things he would have to take with him. They bought him a trunk, which they called a tuck box, that had two little brass locks and his name stencilled on the top. Along with various other things, he packed Bunny, his stuffed toy rabbit with velvet ears, which he kept under his pillow. When he arrived, he immediately noticed that none of the other boys had a teddy, so he maintained that he had lost the key to his tuck box and never opened it. The next year I was sent to the boarding school too. I was the youngest there. My brother had told me various things about the place but nothing could have prepared me for the shock of leaving home. For the whole of that school year, that feeling of fear never completely disappeared. I went from a tiny, two-room village school to a large school run on rigid discipline, Mass every morning, and no visits home for months at a time. The only women were the nuns, who did our laundry; they never spoke, apart from one, the school nurse, whom I tried to see as much as possible.

Years later I realised that the school was barely an hour's drive from our home. It had closed down long ago, but I was told that the chapel had been turned into an Indian restaurant and I proposed to my brother that we should pay a visit, but he dismissed the idea. Once, driving back from Cheshire with an old friend, I suggested we go there for dinner. It was one of those timelessly gorgeous English summer evenings and I could sense the school before it came into view. There was the tall sandstone chapel, lit up in the still-warm sunshine, which was indeed now an Indian restaurant. In my memory, there had been a wall and gates, but it was open to the road now, surrounded by parked cars. At the entrance to the access road I followed a path around the side of the chapel to the back of the building. The playground was now a car park, and the wall with the goalpost painted on it was gone, but the chestnut trees and the low stone wall were still there. Above and around me, the last of the evening light glowed through the foliage, immersing me in an unexpectedly halcyon memory of hurtling around the playground after school. But equally suddenly this idyll vanished, and I felt a draining sensation of school food and polished corridors.

Behind the tall windows on the ground floor was the refectory, separated from the headmaster's office by an arched entrance with double doors, through which we were never allowed. The first-floor windows were the same shape but smaller; these were the classrooms. From my desk, I could see the highest branches of a huge conker tree outside the window. On the top floor in a long room with a vaulted ceiling were the dormitories, with rows of tubular-metal beds along each wall and dormer windows. The boy opposite me wet his bed, and every night a friar would come in just after lights out and escort him to the toilet. Another friar sometimes came in at night to sit beside a certain boy's bed. When my mother asked me, at the end of the year, if anything had happened to me, I was utterly unable to respond.

Inside the chapel, the restaurant had a predictably awkward interior design. I wandered around the back, which had been cordoned off, and there, lining the walls, were the carved wooden alcoves. Every morning I had served as an altar boy for one of the friars, who would say Mass in Latin. On the wall above these pews was a series of old black-and-white photographs of the chapel. The owner of the restaurant saw me photographing them and offered me a drink. When I explained that I had been a pupil at the school, he handed me a small self-published book with old photographs from the 1950s. The dormitory beds were exactly the same, as were the washrooms. Before becoming a Catholic boarding school, it had been a boys' home.

My brother was two years ahead of me at the boarding school and we rarely had any contact, and when we came home for the school holidays we no longer played together in the way we used to. After a year, we were moved to another boarding school, which was run by an order of Irish monks. At the end of the first week, I was taken aside by a monk and caned six times on each hand; apparently it had been my turn to wipe the table after breakfast and I had left it messy. I remember holding my hands under a cold tap to try to numb them, more shocked than in pain. Over the next two and a half years, they beat any belief in religion, authority or education out of me. I went from being top of my class to a kid who shoplifted and smoked; my brother was even worse. Eventually we were both expelled. When my mother came to collect us in our father's car, she told us that this was the most destructive day of her life. I did feel some sense of shame, but an even greater feeling of relief. Maybe she had to believe in the uniforms, the manners, the Latin. I think, when she was much older, the regret caught up with her.

My mother's relationship with my sister was the complete opposite of her relationship with my brother and me. She was so overprotective, she might just as well have bound her feet. My brother and I would try to get our mother's approval by telling her what we had accomplished; my sister got her attention by telling her how badly she had been treated. I remember once when my sister and I were visiting her in the hospital's stroke unit, my mother was propped up in bed wearing an oxygen mask, the heart monitor beeping away in the background. I went down to the shop to buy her a carton of blackcurrant juice, and when I came back, I found my sister telling her at great length about all her problems at work.

One Friday evening, about five years after my mother moved into the home, I was meeting a friend for a drink when my mother rang: she was in the back of an ambulance, being taken to the hospital. She was frantic and implored me to come and fetch her. The carers had found her slumped in a chair, dazed and unresponsive, her face drooping. By the time I reached the hospital, she was asleep on the geriatric ward, so I stayed the night at her house and returned at midday, joining the people being kept waiting for the ward doors to be opened. She could move her arms and, apart from her slightly misshapen face, she seemed unaffected by the stroke. More than anything else, she wanted to go back to the residential home, but the hospital insisted that she remain there until the doctor had seen her on Monday morning. My brother, who worked as a security guard on weekends, would come on the Monday to take her home. I left her on the Sunday afternoon listening to *Gardeners' Question Time* on her headphones.

On the Monday afternoon my sister phoned to tell me that the hospital had discovered a chest infection, which they were treating with antibiotics, and wanted to keep my mother under surveillance for a few days. My brother had seen her and apparently she was fine. It was agreed that my sister would phone the ward each day and relay the news to my brother and me and that my brother would call in to see her during the week. Late Friday afternoon, my brother phoned me and said that he had just seen her and that she looked so bad he did not think she would survive the weekend. I collected my sister and raced up from London in the car, but the traffic was terrible and we missed visiting hours. She was shrunken and grey-faced; her breathing was strained and she looked like she was dying. I went back to the nurses' station and demanded to see the matron, who duly arrived with a lame explanation. My sister and I sat with my mother for a while, my sister holding her hand as she slept, before I informed the matron that we would be returning in the morning. Back at my mother's house, my sister disappeared to her room and I to mine. Unable to sleep, I could not think of any good reason why we should not bring my mother back to the home to die.

The next morning I told my sister what I thought we should do, but the idea frightened her. By chance, a minute or so later, a particularly kind and friendly carer from the home rang to ask how things were, and when my sister told her about our plan to let our mother die in the home, the carer immediately said that they would find a way to help. This reassured my sister, who telephoned my brother, and we arranged to meet at the hospital an hour later. In daylight, my mother looked deathly. I went to the nurses' station and told them that we had come to take my mother back to the home. They fetched the matron, who explained that my mother could not possibly be moved without first being seen by a doctor, and that this being a Saturday, it might be hours before one was available. She added that this would be as good as killing her. I tersely explained that this might very well be the end of their careers; that as far as we were concerned they had almost killed her and that, come what may, we were taking her back to the home. We were shown into a small room and told to wait for a doctor.

We were made to wait for nearly an hour. My sister phoned the home and they said that they were ready to take her back that day. My brother and I agreed that if necessary, we would carry her into my car and drive her there ourselves. Eventually the matron returned with a junior doctor in her late twenties who reiterated the matron's warning, telling me that I would be responsible for my mother's death. My brother and sister looked at the floor, not saying a word. For all my doubts, I was emphatic. The doctor argued back, pointing out that my mother needed intravenous antibiotics and an oxygen machine, neither of which would be available at the home. But I pointed out that she was dying here at the hospital, and we would rather she died in peace in her bed than perish here. 'Listen,' I said to the doctor, looking her right in the eye, 'she's our mother.' This made the doctor tremble and she began sobbing. She said how sorry she was, and that she would do everything she could and that they could lend us an oxygen machine and find an oral alternative to the intravenous medication. After that, nothing was too much trouble and the doctor ran around making all the arrangements. Later that afternoon, when my mother was returned to her room at the home by ambulance staff, the carers were visibly shocked by how much she had deteriorated in such a short time.

She hung on, hovering between sleep and death, the sound of her oxygen machine and the pneumatic mattress the only signs of life. The deacon came and I arranged for her oldest friend to visit. On the Tuesday night, I held her hand and looked at her face, at what remained of my mother, and told her that she did not have to struggle any more: that she had done all she needed to do in this life, that we loved her and that she could go in peace. Early the next morning I walked back to the home and as soon as I came through the doors one of the carers cried out, 'You must go and see your mother!' I rushed along the corridor and there she was, sitting up in bed, putting on lipstick. In more of a croak than a whisper, she told me that she had had a dream in which a creepy doctor had told her it was time for her to go.

E very time something like this happened at the hospital, I would vow I was going to complain, but we would be so exhausted, I never had the energy or the will. But this time I knew I had to do something, so I wrote a detailed letter of complaint to the hospital's chief executive. Before posting it, I showed it to my mother. Because she had been unconscious for most of the time, she had no idea of the extent of her neglect, or how close she had come to dying, and when she read it, she was horrified. I did not want to sue for neglect, but I wanted to make it clear that I expected the chief executive to take responsibility for what had happened. My mother agreed. We demanded that the chief executive visit my mother in the home to apologise and explain what she would do to ensure that this never happened again. The hospital responded with a generic apology and agreed to our demand, but requested that their lawyer accompany her. I refused, saying that if they wanted to include a lawyer, we would too. It was agreed that the chief executive would come with her head of nursing.

All the staff knew about the meeting and the carers made a special effort to ensure that my mother looked her very best. The chief executive began by apologising for the way my mother had been so badly neglected. She told us that she had begun her career in the NHS as a nurse and had worked her way up, and that what had happened to my mother was the absolute opposite of what she had made her life's work. She was clearly very sorry and found it painful to face my mother, who sat there looking old and small. My mother accepted the apology with the grace and sympathy of her generation. To her credit, the chief executive said that she had come to listen to my mother too and asked her what she thought of the hospital. My mother was respectful of authority all her life, but she knew when to speak up. In a quavering voice she said, 'I felt afraid.' Afterwards, I asked my mother what she would like to do and twenty minutes later, sitting in a pub garden, with both arthritic hands and a smile, she raised a half of bitter.

Winters were the hardest times. Travelling took longer, it was more difficult taking my mother out and every Christmas seemed certain to be her last. I would see how some of the other long-term visitors had aged, and I knew I was ageing with them. Sometimes I would be wheeling my mother along a pavement and we would pass a younger man pushing a pram, and I would wonder where my life was going. Week by week, this went on for ten years. By now, she had been there the longest and many of the original carers had moved on. Her eyesight and cognition were so deteriorated, she could hardly read. She had lost so much weight and was physically atrophied to such an extent that if you tried to help her from her chair, she would grimace with pain. The carers had to use a hoist to move her; she would be lifted up in the air like a monkey. The once elegant eighty-year-old who prided herself on her appearance was now in her early nineties with hairs on her chin, and would sit muddled, playing with her fingers, occasionally peering off into the distance, trying to focus. I rarely saw my siblings: my sister and I took it in turns to come up from London, and my brother only ever came during the week. We had all aged badly. Our lives were on hold, warped by the endless visits and constant worrying. We argued over what to do and who was to do it: my brother and I were no longer on speaking terms, and my relationship with my sister was threadbare. I thought they were not doing enough; they thought I was being too controlling. We saw things very differently. Their version of events would be at odds with mine. We had sold her house and almost all the money had gone; the increasingly likely prospect of having to move her because we could no longer afford the home was appalling. All three of us were broke, and if we had to rely entirely on state assistance, it would mean taking her to a low-budget, poorly staffed home and sharing a room. The statutory limit that a local authority would contribute was £375 a week, about a third of her current outgoings. Then came our greatest fear: she was found on the floor of her room, semi-conscious and incoherent. Separately, we all rushed to the hospital.

She was asleep, a plastic oxygen tube across her face, her mouth hollow. Without her dentures, her face had collapsed, while her right cheek was swollen and bruised. The hospital gown had slipped down past her shoulder revealing another huge bruise and two deep grazes as big as the palm of your hand. She looked like she had been beaten up and was unable to speak or respond. The nurse told me that my mother's legs were also badly bruised, so I asked her to show me. She lay there like a helpless child as the nurse gingerly lifted back the sheet and light blanket, inadvertently pulling my mother's gown up past her knees. Although it felt cold-blooded, I knew I must take photographs. Her right leg was one thin, swollen stick, with a series of mottled dark red bruises running from above her knee to her foot. Down her shin were three black bruises, like bullet holes. Both her knees were badly grazed. But it was the sight of her horribly swollen left leg that was so shocking: from her knee to her ankle, there was a marble-black bruise covering her broken skin.

We wanted to know what had happened. The home said that they had found her on the floor, muttering about a squirrel. In a fury, my brother lashed out, accusing them of dropping her. How could someone who could not even sit up in bed fall out of a chair with high arms? We will never know. My mother never recovered. Whatever had happened, it caused massive brain injury. She would be bed-ridden for what remained of her life. I arranged a meeting with the manager of the home who no doubt feared that I would make a forceful complaint, but I knew that would not achieve anything. The best I could do, to help others in the future, was to demand a formal investigation and written report.

Back in the hospital, my mother recovered a little but would have to be moved to a nursing home, and so my sister arranged a meeting with NHS and local authority personnel, in which it would be decided whether my mother's medical requirements satisfied the criteria for awarding her NHS funding, which we desperately needed. Under the regulations, we were allowed to move her to any of the local authorities in which we lived. Given that my sister and I were in London, it seemed obvious that we should move her there. While my brother was able to look after routine errands, he was incapable of dealing with doctors and other care matters and I assumed that my sister would agree that she and I would be the primary caregivers. I spent the next three days researching nursing homes and found one in north London that was easy for my sister to reach on public transport and was just off the bottom of the motorway, so my brother could drive there without having to cross the city. I reserved the room and took along two sets of brochures for my siblings.

I then telephoned my brother, who announced that he would refuse to let my mother move south, which precipitated an argument that ended all further arguments, and we have not spoken since. At the hospital, my sister told me that she did not think our mother could manage the journey to London and that she should go to a local nursing home. When I pointed out that she would be in an ambulance, my sister refused to listen and walked away from me. I had not expected this and, looking back, can only think that either she was unable to side with me and go against my brother's wishes or – as a friend with a similar experience suggested – perhaps she felt that if my mother was close by in London, the responsibility would be too onerous for her.

In the middle of the busy ward, trying to keep my voice to a whisper, I unleashed the most vitriolic condemnation before being sternly interrupted by a nurse who told us that we were wanted in the meeting to assess my mother's medical needs. There were two NHS officials and a social worker from East Cheshire County Council. Niceties over, the senior of the two NHS personnel took charge and proceeded to go through a checklist to establish the severity of my mother's condition, covering criteria such as nutrition, mobility and cognition. Because the NHS is so grossly underfunded and the cost of geriatric care is ballooning, I knew she would try to reject our claim by minimising my mother's needs. The first criterion was breathing. Pointing out her history of bronchial infections, and the fact that she was bedridden, I argued that her needs for this category were high or severe. 'Is she always on oxygen?' countered the official. They looked to my sister. 'Well,' she said, 'I don't think my mother has any real breathing problems.' And then she made a show of diligently consulting her copy of the assessment forms. For the next category, nutrition, I explained that we had to feed my mother with a teaspoon, that her food would have to be pureed and that she could barely eat a child's portion. 'No,' my sister said, 'I bring her home-cooked meals and she eats all of them up.' I might have been putting my thumb on the scale, but my sister was lying through her teeth. The NHS officials were smirking.

The social worker realised what was happening and waited behind after the meeting. She said that because my mother had been in the residential home for such a long time, and given her psychological state, it would cause her great distress to move and so she would see whether, as long as the home was able to make special provision to look after her, the council could negotiate a reduced rate that, topped up by mother's pensions, East Cheshire County Council would fund. This was a lifeline. When I left the room with my sister, I told her that

I was going to go downstairs to the cafe and would wait half an hour before returning to the ward, by which time she must not be there. I had hardly finished my tea when I saw my sister slip past the windows on her way out.

The council was able to reach an agreement with the owners of the home and the manager said, 'Your mother can stay here until the very end.' This was everything I wanted to hear. She never recovered, physically or mentally. Because the hospital had neglected to look after her properly, her right leg had become stuck in a spasm, which had gone untreated by their physiotherapists, so for the rest of my mother's life, it remained bent and uncomfortable. Worse, it meant that she could not be moved out of bed; sitting in a chair, let alone a wheelchair, was impossible. She would never be able to go outside again: she would never smell the air; she would never feel the sun on her face. Cognitively, she drifted between awareness and absence, zoning off somewhere on her own, a here and now full of holes. The carers would bring her exactly the same meals as they served in the dining room, except they were pureed and placed in little moulded sections on a special plate, the vegetables a green or red colour, the meat or pie a beige. They would feed her rapidly with a plastic teaspoon, her mouth covered in smears of food, a wizened infant.

I found going to see her very difficult: how do you visit someone who cannot make a response, who might not know you are there? Sometimes she would recognise me, but she was drifting away. I would bring David Attenborough wildlife films, and we would sit mesmerised by the sound of his voice narrating over the herds of wildebeest and time-lapse landscapes. On better days, I would play her Ealing comedies and she would mouth some of the words. This went on for a year as she slowly disappeared, until eventually she no longer knew who I was, which left me feeling like a ghost. That last winter, one of her close friends died and at the end of the funeral they played a recording of 'Wish Me Luck As You Wave Me Goodbye'. Over the sound of the tannoy you could hear, very quietly at first, her elderly friends singing along, just as they all must have done during the war when their boyfriends and brothers were going away. The next day I visited my mother, taking along a copy of *The Faber Book of Reportage*. I sat by the side of her bed and read an account of children being evacuated from London in 1939. Her eyes opened and her face became animated. I followed this with an eyewitness account from Dunkirk, and again she listened as though it was today's news. Wary of reading something gruesome, I flicked forwards until I came to the ascent of Everest. When I finished with the bit about Tenzing, the Buddhist, leaving behind an offering of sweets, bars of chocolate and packets of biscuits, my mother was beaming and I knew she had come back, if only a little.

From then on, she could recognise me. I brought a book about daily life in London during the war, and we developed a routine with me reading two or three accounts until she fell asleep. She was tired all the time and slept most of the day, like a bony, elderly cat. Her hair had grown wild and she looked berserk. The hairdresser who had a part-time salon in the home would not attend to residents who were bed-bound, so one day I brought along a pair of scissors and asked my mother if she would like me to cut her hair. She had been unable to speak for a long time and looked at me warily, but gave a little nod. I concentrated on her fringe and sides, which I chopped off in big chunks, more worried about safety than style. Finished, I found a mirror and held it up for her to see. Never have I seen her look at anything so intently, and I realised that it was probably the first time that she had seen her face for over a year. She stared at her reflection for a long time, and sighed, and then closed her eyes and sank back into the pillow.

Mid-morning on Tuesday 10 July 2018, the call came. I had seen her on the Saturday; she was feeling so well that they had dressed her in a fancy top and when I had come into her room, she was expecting me. We did a portrait, complete with chopped haircut. The head carer now told me that they found her unconscious just after breakfast and that this time it looked as though she might not recover. I came up straightaway from London and my sister followed that evening. Her eyes were closed and her face was puffy; her mouth was open and her bottom lip was swollen and sagging on the left side. She breathed in slow, shallow cycles: a tiny inhalation and then a long pause, and eventually a weak exhalation. The doctor came and shone a light in her eyes, to which there was no reaction. We met in the manager's office to discuss what to do. Not long after she had moved into the home, my mother had signed a Do Not Resuscitate form, and it was agreed that she would be allowed to die peacefully, without any further intervention, and that if and when the need arose, she would be given morphine. The home told me that they would take care of the arrangements; the deacon came and prayed for her.

The older carers, who had witnessed deaths like this, told me that my mother could last for days, advice I doubted, but found to be true. There were a couple of vacant rooms, where they let my sister and me stay. On the Wednesday night I tried to sit with her all night. The cycles of her breath were even slower, and every time she exhaled, the wait for her to inhale seemed a tiny bit longer and her inhalation a tiny bit weaker. Now and then a carer would quietly come into the room, looking out for me as much as for her. By 6 a.m. I was shattered and accepted an offer to nap in the empty room across the corridor, where I immediately fell asleep, but within minutes I was woken up. My mother had started groaning in pain. I told them to get the morphine, and there was a lot of scurrying around before one of the carers admitted that they had not managed to dispense the prescription for it and there was none on site. They had been so kind to me over the past thirty-six hours, but this was the bitter end. I did not want to appear belligerent, but I made it crystal clear that they had no more than half an hour to get a doctor here with morphine.

I sat on the arm of the chair beside my mother and stroked her hair, and assured her that she would be out of pain soon. Forty minutes later, a grumpy doctor arrived and started asking a lot of screening questions. Bluntly, I ordered him to give her the morphine that instant and when he did, her suffering stopped immediately.

The doctor prescribed her morphine every three hours, which he left instructions for the district nurse to administer. My brother arrived and we sat around in ashen silence. Eventually my sister went back to her own room to wash. I needed a walk and some coffee and left, saying that I would return in half an hour. When I did, my sister was in the corridor, looking for me. My mother was in pain again. She told me that a district nurse was on the way. Incredulous, I found the manager and impressed on her the need to get the morphine now. My mother was moaning loudly, almost like an animal. I held the side of her head in my hand and promised her that I would never leave her side again. Minutes later, the district nurse's assistant came into the room. She wanted to examine my mother and expressed reservations about administering morphine so soon after the last shot. She will never forget my rebuke. I shouted down the corridor for the district nurse, made her give my mother a shot and then sent her out of the room. My brother began looking at his phone while my sister sat in the corner, stunned. I knew that this shot was likely to end her breathing, and sat beside her with my back to the others, stroking her hair very gently, speaking to her in my quietest voice. 'What's the Wi-Fi code?' asked my brother. 'Shhh,' said my sister, 'he's busy with Mum.' Her breathing stopped and remained stopped. I kept stroking her hair and waited several minutes to be absolutely sure, and then said: 'Mum's dead.' ■

June 2013

March 2014

January 2015

August 2016

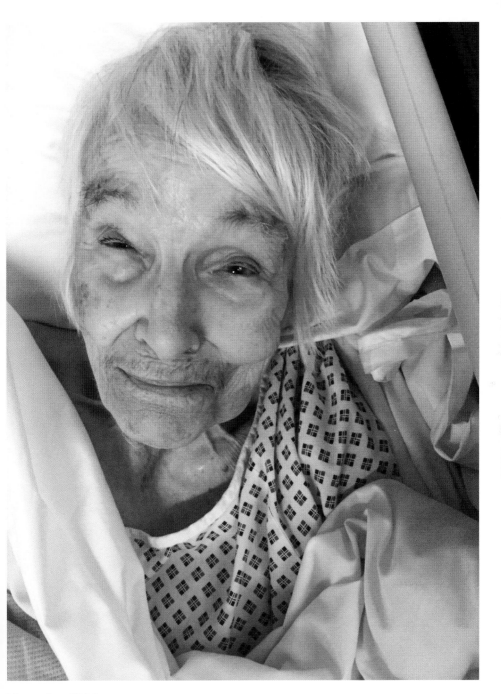

November 2016

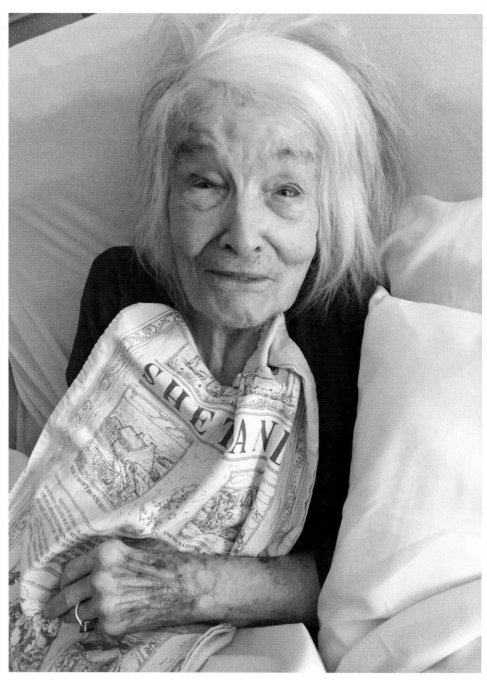

August 2017

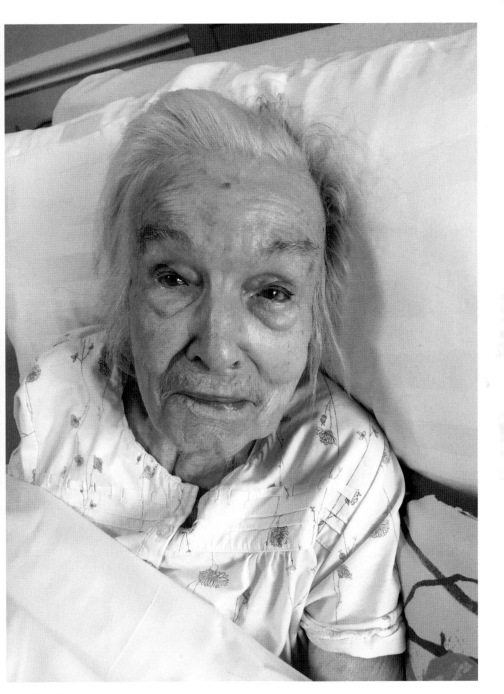

April 2018

July 2018

THE STORY OF ANYA

Mazen Maarouf

TRANSLATED FROM THE ARABIC BY JONATHAN WRIGHT

Disease

Anya had cancer. That was the talk of the whole building. She was ill and would die. But her health never grew worse and she never showed any obvious signs of the disease. Then she suddenly died, without any forewarning. No one expected it to happen like that. Anya and Anya's mother and father all got cancer in the same year. Her father was diagnosed first, her mother some weeks later. Then Anya had similar symptoms and the pain was almost the same, but her parents weren't brave enough to take her to the doctor. They didn't bring the subject up or discuss it. It was all more than they could bear. They preferred not to know for certain, and until they died they acted as if everything was normal. That was in the same year too, a few days apart from each other. Before they died they sent Anya to her mother's brother. Then they died at home and Anya survived. Her mother died first, and her father realised he would follow her soon, very soon, and so he didn't have her buried. He remained lying beside her dead body and that's how they found him.

Everyone in the building shared this story and knew that Anya's uncle had volunteered to bring her up. He was a bachelor and Anya's father was a close friend of his, a friend since childhood. So Anya's uncle loved her doubly, since she was the daughter of a lifelong friend and his sister's daughter. So he was willing to do anything to make sure she didn't come to any harm. He was short and looked like a prehistoric form of human. He spent most of his time making up new fighting methods and combat tricks that could paralyse you, either temporarily or permanently, or that could put you into a highly emotional state – make you laugh or weep hysterically, for example, shock you or terrify you, or whatever. Sometimes courts or police stations would call him in to help them extract confessions from suspects or to uncover the truth. All he had to do was touch the person on the neck or between the eyes. On one occasion a judge asked him to do it in court. It was a complicated case and three judges had already worked on it, one after the other. In the end the court decided to settle the matter once and for all, so they summoned Anya's uncle. The next day his picture was in all the newspapers, which claimed that he was a hero, and he won great respect in our neighbourhood, as though he were an astronomer or a philosopher.

Anya told me he had discovered a way of shaking your hand that could make you freeze like a statue and a way of making you feel pain somewhere in your body whenever you blinked. The pain would turn up in a different place every time. Another of his tricks, she said, was to put pressure on a spot behind your ear and make you lose your hearing in both your ears. Or he could touch a vein in your neck and make you laugh uncontrollably. He was working on a way to stop you breathing until he came and reversed the process, she said.

All these stories about him fascinated me, but we never saw him get into a fight with anyone, except once when he went downstairs and stood outside the building. We realised that something was going to happen because her uncle rarely appeared in public. Then a massive man turned up who we had never seen before. He had obviously come to pick a fight with Anya's uncle, or someone had sent him to take revenge on him for some reason. He spoke with Anya's uncle for some time, and then we saw Anya's uncle suddenly put his hand on the man's shoulder and then push him with his other hand. The man collapsed in a heap on the ground like one of those cardboard boxes that fridges come in. It was the most amazing thing I'd ever seen. We expected the man to get up and pounce on Anya's uncle, because the fall hadn't done him any harm. But he just lay on the ground and, instead of getting up, he burst into tears like a child. We started laughing at him. Anya's uncle left him like that and went upstairs to his flat. Some people tried to help the man get up, but Anya's uncle had put him in a state that meant the more you touched him, the more he cried. Although the people in our building had great respect for her uncle, they kept gossiping about Anya and him. They said that Anya developed cancer in the same year that her mother and father were diagnosed with the disease, that her health was bound to deteriorate and she could die any day. The reason her uncle was always so miserable and nervous was because he was unable to do anything for her, despite his extraordinary ability to mess with people's nervous systems. I had another theory, another story that was completely different – that Anya had cancer because of me.

Sunday 10 August

It was Sunday 10 August when she breathed her last – the hottest day of the year. It happened at noon, the time of day when death can most easily catch people unawares. No one else in the building had an inkling. But on the previous day she told me and Kalashnikov Roses that she was going to die tomorrow. OK, she told Kalashnikov Roses in a whisper while they were hugging and I was standing close by. I had a feeling she was talking about something important that was private to them, so I moved closer and heard everything. Kalashnikov Roses was upset. He tried to break free from her arms, which were around his neck.

'When are you going to stop this nonsense?' he asked.

'Tomorrow,' she replied with a cold smile, as if her heart had stopped beating.

'That's very hard on me,' he said, choking on the words.

'I'm sorry, my dear, but that's what's going to happen,' she said.

She lived on the third floor and her flat overlooked the right-hand part of the car park at the back of the building. Our flat was on the first floor, in the middle, right on the main street. The residents' committee had decided to repair the facade in stages, so it was a building site along the right half at the back. They put up scaffolding all around.

Kalashnikov Roses wasn't from our neighbourhood, but he didn't go home after work that day. Instead, he slept on a scaffolding platform on the fourth floor, where he could look down directly into Anya's bedroom. I think he stayed up late because when I went down to the car park in the morning to see whether Anya had died, as she had said she would, he was still fast asleep. If he had made the slightest movement, even if he had raised his hand to wipe away his tears, he could have fallen to the ground and been smashed to pieces. So he couldn't even cry. He just lay rigid on his right side and looked straight down at her room. He didn't care about the numbness that gradually started to creep up and down his body, starting from the top of his thighs. If that had happened to me, I'd have panicked and groaned for help, but Kalashnikov Roses was made of completely different stuff. In the end he closed his eyes and went to sleep. I slept too that night: I cried for a while but in a muffled way so that my father wouldn't notice. I only stopped when I remembered that on two previous occasions Anya had said she was going to die, but it hadn't happened. When I went down to the car park at the back of the building the following morning to see if there was any sign she had died, it was about seven o'clock. When I looked at her flat I couldn't believe my eyes. Anya was sitting on the balcony reading one of those books that promise to teach you everything quickly, as if they're saying something to the effect of 'Your life will be short'. The book was called *How to Boost Your Self-Confidence in Ten Days*. I stood under her balcony such that I, her line of sight and her book were all in a straight line. I looked at her for a while and then mouthed the words 'Bitch! Whore!' I don't know how many times I mouthed it, maybe ten. I wanted her to see me saying it, but Anya didn't give me a single glance. I thought of shouting out 'Bitch! Whore!' at the top of my voice and then running away so that Kalashnikov Roses wouldn't see me if he woke up. But I went back home instead. As I slammed the door behind me, I could hear my father in the kitchen making his coffee and saying, 'Dog! Pimp!' I thought that if only I could get to sleep for five minutes I would surely dream of Anya, but I didn't know that she was sitting on the balcony because she was waiting for Kalashnikov Roses to wake up and tell her about the dream he had seen her in. When he lay down on the scaffolding platform, the last thing he said to her was: 'I'll dream about you, and in the morning I'll tell you the dream.' So when I went down to the car park I thought Kalashnikov was asleep, fast asleep. But in fact he wasn't: he was just pretending to be asleep. He had his eyes closed just so, and was waiting for me to whistle to give him the secret signal, and then he would know I was going to tell him my dream about Anya. That was because Kalashnikov Roses couldn't have dreams himself, so he had to dream through me. So when I went down and mouthed insults at Anya, he was awake.

'I was aware of you when you came into the car park, but you didn't whistle. I don't know what you did in the car park,' he told me later.

Of course I didn't tell him I'd stood there and mouthed 'Bitch! Whore!' to Anya maybe ten times. But anyway, when I went upstairs to our flat, I went into my bedroom and closed my eyes to go to sleep. I decided that this time I wouldn't tell my dream to Kalashnikov Roses, but to Anya. I would tell her everything – that Kalashnikov had never dreamt of her because he couldn't dream in the first place, and that all the dreams he had told her about were dreams that I had dreamt, not him, and that he had paid me money for this, and I had kept it in a money box, and every banknote had his signature on it, which was a condition I had set because I didn't completely trust him and thought that one day he would hurt me in some way. So I had prepared myself to hurt him and hurt Anya too, even if me hurting her was the last thing that happened to her before she died, because now I was fed up, because Kalashnikov Roses was telling her my dreams in all their detail. He hadn't changed anything.

'Your dreams are wonderful,' he told me. 'There's nothing unnecessary in them, and nothing missing either. They show how much I love Anya. It's not you who dreams them, you know. It's me. But I do it through you.'

Sometimes this would annoy me, but for each dream he paid me well from his job at the workshop. Once I tried to cheat him by making up a dream, just to make more money, but he caught me out.

'I could easily tell,' he said. 'I know you did that because you want more money. From now on, I'll raise the rate for each dream to half my weekly wages.'

Anya told me that his dreams showed how deeply he loved her and that they meant Anya would be his only love. It hurt when I heard that. I resented it, my veins throbbed, I sweated and I wanted to tell her that she was talking about me. But then I would have a nosebleed and when that happened, she and Kalashnikov Roses would make fun of me.

'Look how embarrassed he is. It's like we were talking about him,' she would say.

Sometimes they would speak in great detail about every dream and analyse every detail. Anya found that touching. Her eyes would tear up and she would kiss him on the lips.

My father and all the other people in the building loved Kalashnikov. They said he was very polite despite his rather disturbing name. Maybe it was because he was an orphan, or almost an orphan. In the final days of the war, his mother was on her way to fill two jerrycans with water when a bullet grazed her head. She didn't die, but when she got home she was so frightened she forgot who she was. Her memory started to gradually drain away as her children looked on and in the end she could no longer tell what was what in the house. She looked at Kalashnikov Roses and his brothers and sisters and said, 'Who are you, and where am I?' That frightened them. She opened the door and walked out, and all they could do was watch and cry. That was the last they saw of her.

At the time Kalashnikov had gone out into the street crying. A gunman came up to him and loaded his Kalashnikov. He handed the rifle to him and said, 'Here, let rip with this!' So Kalashnikov picked up the rifle and fired in the air. There happened to be a press photographer with the gunman, but he didn't write a word about Kalashnikov's mother. He took a picture of Kalashnikov shooting and wrote a story about children carrying guns. Kalashnikov Roses had honey-coloured eyes and they were still full of tears at the time. In the picture they seemed to glisten, which made him look more compelling. Anya loved his eyes in the picture. Whenever he kissed Anya, his eyes teared up a little, and she liked that too. Kalashnikov Roses told me it would have been easier if the bullet had gone right into his mother's head and he hadn't seen her leave home in that state. Ever since that day he hadn't been able to dream properly. 'Nothing happens in my dreams,' he said. 'I can't see anything or hear anything. Only one thing happens in my dreams – I feel I'm waiting for someone.'

Dream Bubbles

I don't know how long I slept, but as expected, I saw Anya in a dream. She wasn't in my dream, but in another dream alongside my dream. It was someone else's dream, but I could see everything that was happening in it. In fact my dream not only ran in parallel with that dream, but with dozens of other dreams too. The dreams were packed together like coloured soap bubbles. I realised straight away that everyone who loved Anya was there, each with their dream, and I could see what they were dreaming about her. Some of the dreams were far nicer than my dream. I wanted to be part of them, or to push aside the people who were dreaming them and take their place. I also saw people I hadn't expected. My father was among them, which made me feel embarrassed. I hadn't known he had feelings for Anya, or had even thought about her. It was frightening to discover that, but I was really shocked when I saw Kalashnikov. His dream was right behind my dream, and when I turned around and saw him I felt like someone who suddenly faces a nightmare.

'What are you doing here?' I asked him nervously. 'You're impossible to deal with. Have you forgotten that you can't dream? Wait for me on the scaffolding and I'll tell you everything that happens.'

But because Kalashnikov couldn't see or hear anything in his dreams, I didn't exist as far as he was concerned, neither I nor other people's dreams, which made him relaxed and calm. He just clung to his love for Anya and his sense that she would come to him from other people's dreams and move into his dream. I knew that Anya came and went from one dream to another, like a light moving from window to window, and if she saw him she wouldn't come near my dream, but would go straight to his. I tried to gouge out his dream with my finger to make it disappear, but I was certain I wouldn't be able to do it without breaking the membrane around my own dream, and then I would disappear too, along with him. But it was the only solution since I realised that Kalashnikov wasn't really incapable of dreaming, but was instead waiting patiently for Anya to come to him. I stuck my finger out and advanced towards his dream, but I fell on the ground after two or maybe three steps. When I stood up and tried again, I fell down once more. That's because at that very moment my father was shaking me by the ankle.

'Anya seems to have died,' he whispered, as if revealing a secret.

Anya Moves

The whole building soon found out that Anya was dead. From her uncle. He carried her in his arms like someone carrying a drowned person. He went up and down from floor to floor asking for help. He was barefoot and in such a state of shock that he couldn't find his way to the entrance of the building. Sometimes we heard him saying, 'Please call an ambulance,' but none of the neighbours reacted. They realised that Anya was dead and they were frightened of him. They locked their doors and stayed inside. In the end he sat down on the stairs, hugging Anya and out of breath. He was so tired he could no longer carry her back home. My father had his hand on my mouth and was watching through the spyhole in the door.

'He's sitting on the stairs,' he said.

I was frightened too, so I didn't try to move my father's hand. In the end we heard him going up to the third floor. Even so, none of the neighbours came out of their flats. Everyone decided to pay their respects on the following day. By then her uncle would have got over the shock and calmed down. They were worried that if they went upstairs to offer their condolences, shake his hand, for example, or embrace him, he might touch a nerve in their bodies by mistake and something would go wrong that might be disastrous. Or it might just be something simple, like spending the rest of your life with an itch in your nose.

Our flat was one of the flats that her uncle had kicked during his bout of delirium, right after my father told me that Anya had apparently died. When my father said that, I didn't wake up immediately: I was trying my hardest to get into Kalashnikov's dream and gouge him out with my finger, like removing an egg yolk. But I could hear loud knocking on the front door. I didn't know it was her uncle. It felt like he was kicking me and not the door. I jumped up from where I was asleep on the floor, stared at my father and said, 'What's that?' But my father put his hand over my mouth so that I wouldn't make a sound or cry.

'Shhh,' he whispered. 'Anya's uncle is in a disturbed state of mind. He doesn't even know where the front door of the building is. He went up on the roof and tried to jump down to the street with her. The people in the building opposite shouted at him from their balconies and told him to get down. "The door's downstairs, take the stairs," they said. But he was so upset that after going down a few floors he lost his way, went upstairs again and started kicking on people's doors, but no one responded.'

After my father had checked that Anya's uncle had taken her back to their flat, I opened the door and went downstairs to the car park as fast as I could.

'He's gone upstairs,' my father said. 'Maybe he's trying to bring her back from the dead. Let's wait. Maybe Anya isn't quite dead yet. Don't go out now.'

I paid no attention. I was longing to see her, but I was worried her uncle might still be seriously distraught. He might grab me, for example, in a way that would kill off my love for Anya, or make me uncertain that she had ever existed.

Unexpectedly and without any of us noticing, he left the building with her body late in the evening. I wasn't going to see her funeral or find out where she was buried. If I had known this I might have gone up to her flat and asked her uncle to touch me in such a way that killed off my love for Anya or, in the worst-case scenario, made me uncertain whether she had ever existed. But I ran down to the car park instead, as fast as I could, to check on Kalashnikov. When he humiliated me in front of the other kids in the building, sometimes I would cry and tell him his love for Anya wasn't genuine.

'When Anya dies, we'll find out who really loves her,' I would say.

This time I found he'd climbed down the scaffolding and was sitting under her balcony. He wasn't upset or in tears, but his face seemed to have aged ten years. Some of his hair had even turned grey. As soon as he saw me, he asked in a broken voice why I was late. He said he had had a strong sense that I was going to dream about Anya. That threw me and I lied. I didn't just tell him that I hadn't dreamt of Anya. I also hid from him the fact that I had dreamt of him and had tried to come between them.

'I didn't see her,' I said. 'It was a long, complicated dream. I didn't understand any of it. Then my father woke me up and told me Anya was dead.'

Kalashnikov Roses stared into my face.

'What's up?' I asked.

'I don't know. Nothing about your face suggests you're upset about her death,' he replied. That was true. I thought that maybe I was sad but didn't know it yet. What I knew for sure was that I was confused and felt guilty because I thought I had caused her death.

I didn't know that Kalashnikov Roses would start dreaming again after Anya died, or that I wouldn't dream about her again after that dream. She moved from my dreams to Kalashnikov's dreams, and he would dream about her often, every day in fact. In those dreams she would know everything that had happened to him throughout the day, as if she had lived through it with him, moment by moment. That would make him delirious. Anyway, I would only see him again on one occasion after that. All I know is that after she died she didn't reappear in my dreams.

Whenever I felt I was going to dream about Anya, I would do everything in my power to close my eyes and try to sleep, but to no avail. Sometimes that would happen on my way back from school. I would suddenly stop, lie on the pavement and shut my eyes to go to sleep. That surprised the passers-by and made them curious. A foreign photographer even took a picture of me and published it with an article on meningitis and vaccines for children. But Anya wouldn't appear in my dreams and I felt she was humiliating me. In the end I no longer went to sleep for fear I would wake up frustrated and upset that she hadn't appeared without me understanding the reason. At school I lost my temper with the other kids and became so cranky that everyone avoided me.

I saw Kalashnikov only once after Anya died, when he came to my school during the 12.30 break and stood at the gate. The janitor thought he was the new boy coming to collect the rubbish and told him to come back in two hours. But Kalashnikov waved at me and said he was a friend of mine and wanted to talk to me about something urgently. That was five or six weeks after Anya died. I was amazed at the state he was in. If you'd seen him you'd have thought straight away that he was well on his way to becoming a down-and-out. But he smiled as soon as he saw me. He was moved and there were tears in his eyes. Embarrassed, I went up to him and tried to hide my own emotions.

'What do you want?' I said. 'I haven't been seeing Anya in my dreams since she died.'

'There's no need for that,' he said with a smile. 'She appears in mine every day.'

But I thought Kalashnikov was talking nonsense. He had more grey hair and when he spoke, bubbles of saliva came out of his mouth and gathered on his lip in the corner before bursting. It was embarrassing to be having a conversation with him in front of the other kids. He told me he was now living on sleeping pills and he asked me to lend him some money.

'We could come to visit you in a dream if you want, like in the old days,' he said. I had the impression he felt sorry for me. He reached out over the wall to touch my head but I backed away. I told him I would pay back all the money he had given me for the dreams. He could meet me in the car park after school and I'd give him the money box.

In the car park he told me that Anya came to him in his dreams every night. Although he enjoyed it, it did confuse him. He felt it was a figment of his imagination and there was something wrong with his mind.

'Even if I loved her that much, it doesn't make sense to dream about her every day,' he said.

It couldn't just be a matter of dreams. There was something inexplicable about it, something deeper, that went further.

'All you can do is assure me that it's not just a matter of dreams and that Anya lives with me in this life during the day, and then she lives with me in a parallel life during the night,' he said.

'Me? Why bring me into it?' I asked, pretending not to care.

'She told me you made a wish that she would get this disease, that you did that after you saw her kissing me in the junk room,' he said. 'Is that true? If it's true then it's not just a matter of dreams.'

I felt my blood was boiling then. It was clear that something really unusual was going on between him and Anya. Exceptional. Maybe she didn't just appear in his dreams, but they went off to a parallel life together every night. But I saw it as my chance to get revenge for everything they had done to me. I remembered how they had made me scrape up the shit in front of Anya's flat and how he would lie in wait for me to extort my dreams in exchange for a little money, and how they made me come along with Kalashnikov when he was meeting her, as if I were their pet dog. Now I wanted to pounce on him and punch him, and send him back to Anya in pieces.

'No. That's not true,' I said. 'I didn't wish anything on Anya. Anya was ill before. She got the disease in the same year as her mother and father. The whole building knows that. Ask them.'

Kalashnikov Roses was looking at the money box and tossing it from hand to hand.

'She also told me that the day she died you saw her in a dream, and you saw me too, but you tried to come between us,' he continued. 'But I don't know. Maybe I can't see her in my dreams and it's my mind that's inventing the whole story. In the end you aren't bold enough to have done that. But I don't know. Maybe you told her that. Or maybe my mother's the reason. If someone goes mad, they take with them at least one member of their family too.'

As he said this I was thinking about one thing – asking if I sometimes appeared in his dreams with him and Anya. But he turned and walked away without saying another word.

'What? Don't you believe me?' I said, but he didn't answer. That was the last time I saw him. I didn't know that a few days later he would decide to hole up in one of the buildings abandoned because of the war, swallow a bottle of sleeping pills, and go into a coma for weeks until his body dried up and he died. I saw his picture in the newspaper. They found him while they were laying explosives in the building to prepare it for demolition. They placed an advert asking anyone who recognised him to pick up the body from the morgue in the government hospital. Then Anya's uncle turned up and took his body away. With Kalashnikov's death, I hoped that Anya would reappear in my dreams, but it didn't happen.

The Police Station

When Kalashnikov appeared and told me that Anya said I had laid a curse on her, I felt I had caused her death. So I went to the police station and went up to the policeman standing by the door.

'I want to confess,' I said.

'Confess what?' he asked.

'I killed a girl called Anya. She was fourteen years old.'

I was held for questioning, but less than forty-eight hours later they released me. It wasn't easy. The sergeant flew into a rage and decided to teach me a lesson. It's not that he slapped me in the face, for example, or hung me upside down till my guts fell out of my mouth. He told me he could have done all that to me, but he had found a better method. He was meant to go to hospital to see his wife give birth to their first child. But when the policeman told the sergeant that someone had come to confess to killing a child, he had to stay in the station. In the morning he had Anya's medical file in front of him.

'The papers here say that Anya died of the disease she had. But if you insist you killed her and you want to be punished, then that's no problem as far as I'm concerned. But first, tell me, do you feel any remorse for what you did?' he said.

'Yes, I am remorseful,' I said.

'Why haven't I seen you crying then?'

'I don't know. I haven't cried since she died. I don't know why.'

'You're meant to have tears, and lots of them too. Because you need tears now. They're the only thing that's going to get you out of this police station.'

On the morning of the next day the sergeant made me clean the bathroom in the police station – the toilets, the basin, the tiles on the floor and the walls, and even the policemen's boots.

'I gather you have no problem scraping up shit,' he said.

When he waved his hand, Tuxedo appeared. I couldn't control myself. Tears streamed from my eyes. Tuxedo looked at me and then went into the bathroom. After that the sergeant said, 'Now we've made a start. Now I want you to cry and never stop crying. Can you see the bathroom? I want you to wash it with your tears, not with water.'

I don't know how many hours that took me. I had to keep crying but in the end, after the sergeant went off to hospital, one of the policemen took pity on me.

'Use water,' he said. 'But hurry up before the sergeant comes back.'

When I left the station on the evening of the second day, my eyes were red and swollen and painful from all the crying. But I thought that even if I went blind I deserved what had happened to me. Because Anya had died because of me. Because I had wished cancer upon her, and then she had got it. It all happened the first time I tried to kiss her. She was two years older than me, and she hadn't yet met Kalashnikov Roses.

'OK,' she said, 'but do it like a man. If you know how to kiss me, I'll let you kiss me every day.'

When she said that, the first thing I thought of was a kissing scene in the whisky advert. Anya took me to the junk room on the third floor of the building. In the junk room you could hide without anyone seeing you. You could squeeze in between the piles of unwanted furniture and boxes and so on. There was space for two people, but only in a sitting position. You found yourself surrounded by all kinds of discarded things – kitchen stuff, broken toys, old chairs and other clutter. Anya was a little taller than me, maybe an inch. She leaned towards me and said, 'Now I'm going to shut my eyes and you kiss me. OK? Shut your eyes as you do it. It's better that way.'

'OK,' I said. I shut my eyes but Anya kept hers open. I was very embarrassed at the time. I know that. So much so that I felt my blood pumping right through my body and gathering in all the veins in my face. As I put my lips close to her cheek, my nose started bleeding. She clasped her hand to her chest, pushed me away and moved back a little.

'Your nose is bleeding,' she said. I put my hand on my nose to check. There really was blood. It had stained my fingers and my sweater. I'd never had a nosebleed before. It felt as if the temperature of my body had fallen, and I started to shake, thinking it meant I was going to die. I thought I would fall down, my blood would drain out among the clutter and I would breathe my last.

'Tell my father,' I said in a panic.

'There's no need for that. Go downstairs, wash your nose and lie down a while till the bleeding stops,' she said, shaking her head coldly. She dragged me out of the junk room by the arm and escorted me to the top of the stairs. I went downstairs, into our flat, entered the bathroom, washed and then lay down on the sofa, maybe for half an hour. I went back up to the junk room as soon as the bleeding stopped. Anya wasn't there any longer. I waited maybe an hour, but she didn't come back.

Nosebleeds

That was my problem with Anya. Whenever we were alone together I was so embarrassed that blood immediately started running out of my nose. It didn't just run: it poured out in two wide streams, and without warning too. It was like being hit on the head with a baseball bat. I couldn't stop it or even reduce the rate of flow, and it made a big mess. My hands and clothes were covered in blood, and that disgusted her. It gave the impression I was in pain and not just embarrassed. At school she told me my blood was very red, as if it had come straight from my heart.

'If you go on like this, you'll have anaemia,' she said.

Anya was the smartest kid in the class. She wasn't unusually beautiful. When I looked at her face at length, it grew less attractive with time. She faded, as if her magic had abandoned her and dispersed in the air in tiny fragments. I told myself this meant my nose wouldn't bleed if I met her at school that day. I couldn't tell her I'd discovered that she lost her attractiveness when I looked at her for a long time, and that meant I was no longer embarrassed. But when we were alone together, something different happened. She regained her magic – in fact it was like seeing her for the first time.

'At school you told me you wanted to tell me something important,' she said. 'What was it?'

Before I could say a word, the blood had rushed to my face and started pouring out of my nose. Then in school she would come to me and say, 'Your face is pale today. It's probably because of your nosebleed yesterday. Did it bleed for long at home?'

'No,' I said. 'The bleeding stopped as soon as I got home.'

'Good, and what did you want to tell me?'

'I wanted to tell you that if I look at your face for a while when my nose is bleeding, then the bleeding will stop,' I said.

'And how do you know that?'

'I know!'

But she never gave me that opportunity. The sight of blood was more than she could bear. It reminded her of her parents' death, though she had never seen them bleed. In fact they were far away when they died. They were sad, and they each died alone. That's what they'd agreed. That the first to die would die alone so that the other person wouldn't see them. And she was staying with her uncle when they died.

There were small scars on Kalashnikov Roses's face. He looked like the villain in one of those old movies. He got the scars from working in the workshop with my father. Kalashnikov started in the workshop as a boy. He was skilled at cutting glass, but splinters would fly off and get in his face. Eventually a large piece hit his face. It didn't go deep or anything. It just made a scratch, but it was one of those scratches that leaves a mark. It was the doctor who decided to press a lawsuit against my father. After treating Kalashnikov Roses, the doctor made a phone call from his clinic. The judge was a friend of his. In the meantime my father and Kalashnikov were waiting in the corridor for the doctor's report. The court case didn't take long. In a single session the court ruled that Kalashnikov was entitled to one year's leave on the same pay he had been earning, as compensation for the scars on his face. After the one year Kalashnikov would be entitled to go back to the workshop if he wanted. There wasn't a second session and my father didn't hire a lawyer. But he felt that the ruling was totally unfair. So Kalashnikov Roses got paid by my father at the end of every month.

My father often spoke about him – how he had taken Kalashnikov on soon after his father had died, and other details. I knew everything about Kalashnikov Roses, but I had never seen him until that day when he came to our flat. My father had decided to take me to the doctor after my repeated nosebleeds. I was too embarrassed to tell him it only happened when Anya and I were alone together, so I suggested that instead of going to the doctor, we ask Anya's uncle to treat me. Just one of his touches might cure me. But my father said, 'Anya's uncle can't treat you unless he knows how you feel when you have a nosebleed. You'll have to tell him what you feel just before it starts. Otherwise it won't work.'

So I wasn't able to make use of her uncle's talents. I wasn't going to tell him that it happened when I was about to kiss Anya or that it was because I was embarrassed. If I'd done that he might have grabbed me in a way that left me with my mouth open for ages, and I would no longer be able to control my saliva, which would slobber down my chin all the time. I had dreamt about that, and even I was disgusted. So the only solution was to have a third person with us when we were alone, and then my embarrassment would go away and I could kiss her. I saw Kalashnikov that day and he seemed very polite and even apologised to my father for the court ruling. My father said, 'It was nothing to do with you. That doctor's a son of a bitch,' adding that Kalashnikov deserved a year off work anyway since he hadn't had a holiday since he had started work in the workshop. So I thought to myself that Kalashnikov was exactly right to be with Anya and me.

When I first introduced him to her, I didn't feel there was anything strange. I had primed myself to say, 'My nose won't bleed today. Do you want to try?' But she was talking to Kalashnikov all the time and she didn't exchange a word with me. They spoke about their lives and laughed together. She patted him on the shoulder once and asked him if he would be coming back to the building. He said that of course he would come, and so they began to date. Everything happened fast. When I first saw them kissing in the junk room, it was by chance. I had been spying on them. They were seated and Anya kissed him with her eyes closed. He did the same to her. I stood there expecting Kalashnikov to have a nosebleed, but it didn't happen. When I went up to her at school the next day, I was so upset that I said, 'I hope you get cancer.' I didn't know anything specific about the disease but I had often heard the children at school talking in awe about the most frightening diseases in the world, such as kidney failure, cancer, strokes, hepatitis, anaemia and piles. Even the science teacher had an opinion on the subject.

'Cancer is the strongest disease in the world. It's so strong that if you wish it on anyone, they'll get it,' he said. I didn't pay much attention to what the teacher said at the time. I didn't imagine for a moment that I would not only wish it on someone, but wish it on Anya of all people. Two or three weeks later people in the building started saying that Anya had the disease and was going to die. I felt guilty from the start: that I was the cause, because I had laid a curse on her.

'I hope your uncle punishes me even harder than he did when I went upstairs to your flat at dawn,' I said, but her response was, 'Are you stupid? Do you think I'd get cancer because you wished it on me? I had it before you even learned to speak.' But even if she had had the disease because of me, her condescending attitude would have prevented her from admitting it. She would have felt humiliated if a nonentity like me had wished her ill and it had worked. She said she and her parents all got the disease in the same year.

How I Protected Anya's Uncle

No one dared ask Anya about her mother and father. That was because of her uncle. Everyone was afraid of him, even the local thugs that the army wanted nothing to do with. But one of them did challenge him in the billiards hall. His name was Tuxedo. He bragged that he had such calm nerves that Anya's uncle couldn't put him out of action. They had an arm-wrestling match. It's true Tuxedo won, but Anya's uncle didn't care about winning. While Tuxedo was tensing his muscles, Anya's uncle pressed his thumb into a spot on Tuxedo's hand, and ever since then Tuxedo has been waking up at four in the morning with a terrible stomach ache and desperate to have a shit. He realised that Anya's uncle had got the better of him.

When the stomach aches had sapped his strength and all the stomach medicines and special diets had failed to bring relief, he decided to force Anya's uncle to fix the problem. He started turning up at dawn in his blue Buick with a couple of other cars full of gunmen. He would get out while the others waited outside the building. He would go up to the third floor alone, and then to Flat 37 at the end of the corridor. At exactly 4 a.m. he would take down his trousers, squat, empty his bowels at the door, and leave. Anya's uncle got the message. But he decided not to confront him in the hope that Tuxedo would give up. Or maybe he was afraid Tuxedo would do something bad to Anya in revenge. All he did was pretend to be asleep. But Anya was the problem.

When she opened the door to go to school, she found Tuxedo's shit right in front of her. She went down the stairs terrified and pale-faced. If someone did that, it meant they were threatening her uncle. She went home and said she didn't want to go to school again. She wanted to stay home, protected by her uncle. He reassured her. From then on he took her by the hand, went downstairs with her and stayed till the taxi driver he had hired arrived and she went off to school. Anya would implore him to look after himself. Once I saw her crying at school. I would only see her during break because she was two classes ahead of me. I told her I would protect her uncle. I could skip school to protect him, two or three days a week, because just as Anya was the smartest kid in her class, I was the smartest kid in mine and I had a reserve of extra marks in most subjects. I'd sit on the third floor outside their door even if there was shit everywhere.

'Do you really want to do that?' Anya said.

'Yes.'

'But you'd have to remove all that stuff first.'

'Yes, I'd remove it first and then protect the house,' I said.

'No, I'd like you to remove it before I go to school. I'd be happy if you did that,' she said with a smile. I couldn't believe my ears. I promised her I would start that night.

'And I'll wake up to spy on you through the spyhole in the door, to see if you're really going to do it,' she said.

So I would wake up a little before four in the morning and, after Tuxedo's convoy of cars had left, I would go upstairs on my tiptoes, with a putty scraper, two plastic bags and a cardboard box, to scrape up the shit. I didn't use the scraper. It was more like a weapon, just in case. My father left all his tools in the workshop, except for the scraper, which he always brought home with him. Since my mother died, he hadn't left a single knife loose in the flat before he went to sleep. He put them all in his wardrobe and locked it. My father never told me how my mother had died, but I gathered from this habit of his that her death had something to do with kitchen knives and other sharp implements. So I chose one of them as my weapon against Tuxedo if he should turn up unexpectedly.

That's why Anya and Kalashnikov Roses later called me Scraper. I couldn't stand the name, but I eventually got used to it. Sometimes Anya would make fun of me and she and Kalashnikov would say that the name suited me perfectly since I was so good at scraping up other people's shit without leaving a trace, not even the smell. Tuxedo's shit was as big and heavy as rhinoceros shit, and every morning I went to Anya's door, scraped it up and threw it into the broken lift. The neighbours were annoyed by the smell, which spread to all the floors in the building. But nobody dared complain. I didn't know that Anya's uncle had offered to make up with Tuxedo and cure his ailment, provided Tuxedo came and removed all the shit from inside the lift. This made Tuxedo angry, but he didn't have any other option, and her uncle felt that in this way he had regained status and respect.

Tuxedo wouldn't find out it was me who had done that until later, at the police station after Anya had died.

Later, after Anya met Kalashnikov Roses in the junk room, she would wait till her uncle was asleep and let him in on the sly, and they would do things. She loved his bravado. No one else was bold enough to go into her uncle's flat like that. But in fact it was Anya who would have defended Kalashnikov in front of her uncle if he had found out he was there. Her uncle couldn't refuse in case he upset her and her health grew worse. Maybe her uncle knew about it. When I asked her, she told me Kalashnikov guarded her uncle inside the flat and I guarded him outside, and I believed that. Sometimes when I was scraping up the shit, Anya and Kalashnikov were kissing and touching each other behind the door. I could hear the sounds they made. They would spy on me while I was scraping up the shit and laugh into their hands. Then they would do more kissing and fondling.

In the meantime I started skipping school. I would sit on the floor outside the door to Anya's flat until her uncle woke up at nine o'clock or half past nine in the morning. As soon as I heard him I'd get up and rush home. The condition Anya set was that her uncle shouldn't notice I was protecting him. So a couple of days after I started scraping up the shit and skipping school to protect her uncle, Anya told me to wait for her in the junk room because she wanted to try something else out with me. That was when she offered to let me kiss her. She said girls could fall in love with a man at first kiss rather than at first sight. The first kiss decided everything.

'Do it like a man,' she said.

After I had the nosebleed she told me I wasn't ready to kiss a girl yet, but she would wait for me. But she didn't wait at all, because days later she met Kalashnikov Roses and she kissed him in front of me. OK, I wasn't supposed to see them: I was snooping on them. They were in the junk room and I was waiting for Kalashnikov to have a nosebleed, but it didn't happen. When they'd finished she said 'Oooof' in a soft voice, as if she were submitting, then he kissed her again, passionately.

Shit Your Spit

My hope that Anya would fall in love with me was tied to Tuxedo's shit. I didn't realise this until Tuxedo gave in and made peace with her uncle. I kept going up to the third floor a little after 4 a.m. as usual, with a cardboard box, two bags and the scraper. I'd look for Tuxedo's shit, not just outside Anya's flat but all along the corridor, right and left. I scraped the whole floor with the cardboard box and sniffed it tile by tile like a dog because the corridor was dark during the frequent power cuts. When I couldn't find anything, I'd knock on the door and whisper, 'Anya, Anya, have you seen any shit?' But no one answered. I was desperate. I waited for the Buick to arrive with Tuxedo in it. Then at school one day Anya told me her uncle no longer needed me or my protection. I started going up to her door at exactly 4 a.m., on tiptoe of course. Outside her door I pulled down my trousers and shat, leaving a turd that was smaller than Tuxedo's turds of course. Then I went back home and waited for Anya to come and ask me for help. But she didn't speak to me. So when my patience was exhausted, I asked her, 'Didn't you find a piece of shit outside your door today?'

She looked at me in amazement. It was the first time I had seen her eyes throwing sparks like that.

'OK then,' I said, 'I very much suspect it was Kalashnikov Roses who did it.' I couldn't tell if she knew I had done it.

'Yes, I find shit every day and I clean it up myself,' she said distractedly.

At 4 a.m. the next day I went up to her door as usual. I turned my back on the door, squatted down and did it. Then I went home. About half an hour later I came back with the cardboard box, the two plastic bags and the scraper. I wanted to tell Anya that I was there and that I had come to clean everything up. And this time I would protect her. My plan was to knock on the door and whisper, 'Anya, Anya, I'm here, and I've come to clean up the shit.' But there was nothing there.

I might as well have shat air. So I knocked on the door and whispered, 'Anya, Anya, did you see the shit?' But suddenly her uncle opened the door, with one of those box-cutters in his hand.

'What are you doing here, you prick?' he said. I tried to stay as cool as Kalashnikov Roses, Tuxedo and the other local thugs.

'Isn't there supposed to be some shit outside your door?' I said.

'No, but now there'll be some outside your door,' he replied. He grabbed me by the scruff of my neck and took me down to our flat. Then he pulled down my pyjama bottoms with his other hand and forced me to squat.

'Shit!' he said. But my bowels were empty, nothing in them at all.

'My bowels are empty,' I told him.

'That's not my problem,' he said. 'You've got to shit. And I want it to be a big shit, like rhinoceros shit. Otherwise I'll have your brain come out of your nose.'

I started to squeeze as hard as I could. My father was standing behind the door but he didn't dare open it. Later he told me he had wanted to teach me a lesson, but I know he was frightened of Anya's uncle. After about half an hour maybe, a small piece of shit came out. My father was spying on me through the spyhole in the door. I started crying and pleading with Anya's uncle. I told him there was nothing in my bowels but spit.

'Shit spit then,' he said.

I squatted like that till I heard Anya calling him and saying, 'That's enough.'

A Suicide in Soundproof Glass

It's true that after she died Anya no longer appeared in my dreams, but I found a way to see her whenever I wanted. At first it was easier, and later it took me longer. Even so, I was satisfied in the end. My father thought that what I was doing was making suicide attempts. He tried to persuade me to stop. He had never been close to me, but now he would sit on the edge of my bed every morning and talk to me. Sometimes he said trivial things, just for us to be close. Sometimes he would say, 'How about I tell you a secret and you tell me one in return?' And before I could answer, he would be telling me about the mistakes he made in his relationship with my mother. When he'd finished, I'd tell him I didn't have any secrets.

'OK, then tell me just one thing. Are you going to make a suicide attempt today?' he asked.

'I don't know,' I replied, because I really didn't know.

But my father was willing to do anything to distract me.

'Even the workshop, I could have it registered in your name. Ask for anything. The important thing is you don't do it again.'

I had explained to him several times that with my suicide attempts I didn't mean to kill myself.

'Only my first attempt was meant to do that. I admit it. All the other attempts were for other reasons,' I said. This made my father even more confused.

'Your mother used to say the same thing all the time. Her repeated attempts to kill herself wore me down. Seeing her pick up a knife, or stand by the window, or go into the bathroom and lock the door was enough to make me very anxious. In the end I couldn't take it, and when she packed up and left, I just looked on.'

After my third suicide attempt my father was about to lose his mind. He said, 'The doctor in the emergency ward tells me that every time they try to resuscitate you, your dick is erect. We both know you're still young. If you want sex films I'll get you some. The doctor said it might be some kind of sexual disorder.'

I kept telling him I didn't need anything, and if I did need anything I would get it and not commit suicide. But when I think about it now, after all these years, I don't think I should have made so much effort for Anya's sake, because the chances of her loving me depended on a piece of shit. You can imagine how deep love must be when it's a piece of shit that has brought two people together. But Anya went on loving

Kalashnikov Roses. Instead of trying to win her over, I did my best several times to convince Kalashnikov that his love for Anya wasn't genuine and his feelings were just a figment of his imagination. But Kalashnikov, who was a simple lad and sometimes got easily confused, said, 'I don't know if I have any imagination. I can't dream, at least.'

The most I could do was make him doubt for a while that he loved Anya. Then he settled the matter by saying, 'All I know is that when I think of her and touch my face, I no longer feel it has scars.'

My father had a small workshop that made soundproof glass and he always came home in dirty overalls. The window units had two panes of glass with a vacuum between them. Soundproof glass was common after the war. Despite all the assurances, people weren't confident that the war had ended irreversibly. They were tired of sticking the glass together all the time whenever the sound of an explosion or a distant shell made cracks in it. My father made the window units at low cost from materials that would crack instead of splintering, reducing the sound level when an explosion took place. But he was the only person in the building who didn't install soundproof glass in his own flat. He preferred to keep the ordinary glass because that way he could hear people scream whenever I made another suicide attempt. But people took it as a sign that he didn't trust his own products, and so they went to other factories.

'You do realise that your suicide attempts have led to massive losses at our factory?' my father said. We had moved to another building in another area.

I wasn't lying to my father. On my first attempt at suicide I really did intend to die. I did that shortly after I saw Kalashnikov Roses for the last time, after he took the money box from me. I was angry at finding out that Anya had moved from my dreams to his, and I wanted to die so that I could be with them when she appeared to Kalashnikov in his dreams. First I thought of climbing up the scaffolding and jumping, but that would have left bruises, or my neck would have broken like a matchstick, or my skull would have been crushed. That meant I would appear deformed in Anya and

Kalashnikov's dreams. So I thought up another way of killing myself – by giving myself a hernia. That wouldn't leave any marks. The local lads used to play basketball in the car park, and I went up to one of the cars there, put my hands under it and tried to move it. I knew I wouldn't be able to do it, but the aim was to lift a heavy weight for so long that my insides split and I died in a faint on the spot, with blood running out of my nose. I felt the hernia developing inside me, like buttons being torn off a shirt. I kept trying to lift the car while the guys in the car park began urging me on, chanting, 'Scra-Per! Scra-Per! Scra-Per!' They were about to start betting on me when I fell to the ground. I was no longer aware of anything. At that moment Anya appeared. It's true that I fell on the back of the car first and then to the ground, but it felt like a fall from the top floor of the building. I was in tremendous pain and felt a burning sensation in my legs and arms and throat. For a moment I thought it had worked and death really does take you from this life to the world of other people's dreams, and you can spend your life roaming from dream to dream, sometimes in human guise and sometimes as a plant or a noise or even a backdrop. That way you would never feel bored because your life would be constantly changing. But I didn't see Kalashnikov Roses anywhere, and because it's impossible to have a dream without being present in it, I realised things weren't as I had thought, especially as Anya told me to drop dead. She didn't use those exact words, but something inside me was certain that this was what she was saying. In the same way as in dreams, when you can understand something without any spoken reference to it.

'You're dead, and all you have do is say "I hand over my soul to you" and your soul will shove off,' she said, offering me an open paper bag like the sick bags on a plane, with the difference that it had a recycling logo on it. It's true what she said. I was dead as far as the doctors were concerned. I didn't have a pulse. But Anya seemed to be in a hurry, because Kalashnikov Roses was waiting for her and she had to go back to him.

'Even if you're really and truly an angel, you're always in the same mood – a bad mood,' I said, but Anya didn't even recognise me. She didn't know who I was or what I was talking about. I sensed that, but she wasn't interested and seemed a few years older. That was the first time I felt I didn't need to make so much effort for her sake. I felt so humiliated. I felt as if her uncle's fingers were pressing on my neck as they had done when he said, 'Shit your spit.' My heart stopped beating for a moment that day, but I didn't hand over my soul and I came round later. When I had told Anya and Kalashnikov about her uncle's fingers, they had made fun of me. And when I woke up in the resuscitation room the doctor proudly told me, 'We lost you for about a minute, but real heroes make a comeback.' When the local lads later asked me what I had seen, I said that when the angel of death comes to take our souls, he comes in the guise of the person we've loved most in our lives. That eases the pain and maybe distracts us from it. And maybe my own angel of death would look like Anya.

Hospital

The last time I saw her, she was pregnant. I couldn't believe it. Seven months had passed since my last suicide attempt. She looked quite exhausted, as she was going to give birth soon. I realised that whenever I evoked her in my dreams she came to me from Kalashnikov Roses's dreams, and it was a long distance between me and Kalashnikov. Even so, I associated her exhaustion with her disease, not with her pregnancy. For the first time you could look at her and feel there was something wrong with her physically. She was tired, thin and sweating. She stood in front of me, however, with the same grace and self-confidence, and said, 'You're dead now. All you need to do is say "I hand over my soul to you" and it'll automatically shove off.' As usual, Kalashnikov Roses wasn't around, but I had a hunch that he had the same disease now and was in a bad way. That meant I wouldn't be able to summon her up in my dreams any longer, because he was in his last days and she would be spending the time beside him. I wanted to go up to her and help her sit down. For the first time I felt like a brother to her, not a boy who was obsessed with her. But I couldn't take a step towards her.

'I'll wait till you give birth and then I'll drop dead,' I said.

I would stay around to look after her baby girl, and I was sure it would be a girl, and I would take care of it. That might happen in an hour, or two hours, or at the end of the day at the latest. And I would have no problem with that, given that I could stop my heart beating for hours through practising suicide and repeatedly coming back to life. While I was thinking about all this, I realised I was in hospital, just like every time, with the difference that I was waiting outside the room, in the emergency department, sitting next to other fathers of all ages. But none of them seemed to notice I was there. While I was listening out for a newborn baby to scream, there was a sound from another room – a doctor telling an anguished father, 'We did everything we could. This time we really seem to have lost him. Don't cry, because his soul might still be around.' I was afraid to look up to see the father who came out of the room just at that moment. He was wiping his tears away with the sleeve of his dirty overalls. ∎

THAT'S GOOD.
SO
CAN I GET YOU ANOTHER DRINK?
NAH MATE, I SHOULD BE GETTING HOME.
ARE YOU RIGHT TO DRIVE? I CAN CALL A CAB.
I'LL BE FINE, THANKS STEVE.
THANKS ANDREW, SEE YOU TOMORROW.
YEAH~ SEE YOU TOMORROW.

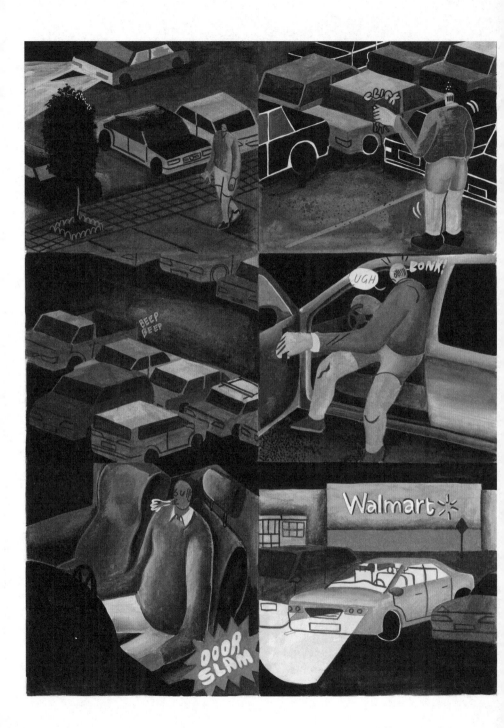

YOU SEE, THE RHYTHM OF CHEMICALS CYCLING IN THE HUMAN BODY IS MAINTAINED BY FAINT ELECTROMAGNETIC SIGNALS GENERATED BY EARTH'S ELECTRONS.

YOU MAY RECEIVE A DOSE AT THE BEACH WHILE WALKING ALONG THE WET SAND OR STANDING ON A DEW-MOISTENED LAWN. FOR MANY PEO~

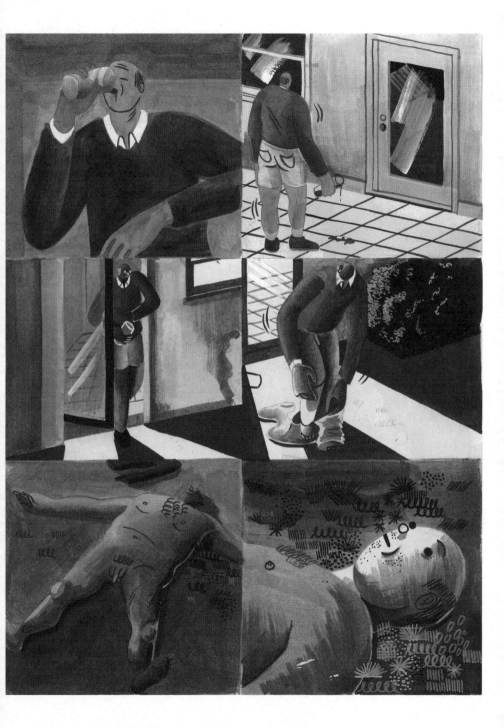

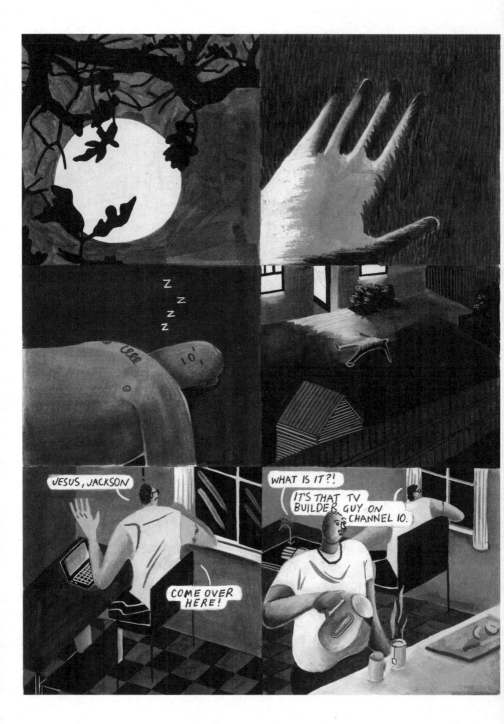

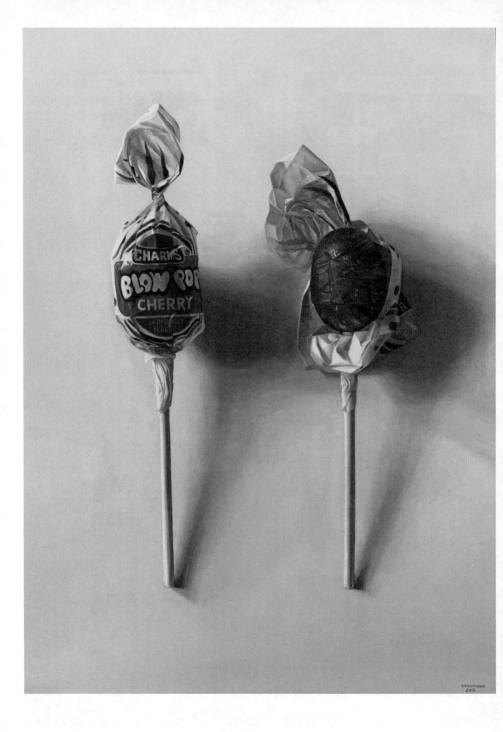

© GINA MINICHINO
Two Blow Pops, 2018

THE YOUNG
ENTREPRENEURS OF MISS
BRISTOL'S FRONT PORCH

Sidik Fofana

And you know how Bernita is. Making jokes about people so everybody still know she the Queen Bee. 'Cept everybody else get they jokes to they face. She go behind Kandese back to clown her. Kandese say one of them New York phrases like that's OD or it bees like that and Bernita wait til we leavin the porch for the day and start makin fun of the way she talk, sayin she sound like a man.

Now look at her ringin Miss Bristol bell, crackin jokes before Kandese come out. Narely she jus go along. She crackin up, snortin and shit, tryna get me to laugh, too, so Bernita don't get mad. Bernita go to Narely and say that's funny, right? and punch her on her shoulder hard, and Narely automatically start laughin harder. Bernita lookin at me tryna to get me to laugh, tryna sound hoarse like Kandese. Her fat ass is on the railin tryna lean on it, but she eyin me to make sure I laugh so she be happy and know she still the Queen Bee of the South. But she know I know her secret. She know she been makin fun of people to they face ever since we was all at the cafeteria at Ida B. Wells and the lunch muhvas wasn't lookin and the other girls was sayin ooooh. She know Kandese the only girl who don't get her jokes to her face, that she the only girl Bernita trade lip gloss with say hey girl to. She know I heard her the one time she ask Kandese what we was gonna do with our money and Kandese said let me handle it and Bernita said okay. She know the only reason I ain't say nothin to her about any of that is because she got a rep. But reps only go so far. Specially when you can see right into someone's gut and you realize the stuff they got in it ain't as tough as you thought.

Hehe, hehe, I go and she keep tryin harder, scrunchin up her face like Kandese do and talkin with her fingers like Kandese, but all I see is Bernita's overweight self and that extra skin on her booty hangin over the top of her jeans and her stubby fingers and the nasty spit comin out the corners of her mouth and I get mad at myself for even givin her the hehe. And she know that too. She know unless Kandese hearin these jokes, she ain't foolin nobody.

The screen door pop open and Kandese come out with all the candy and that long m-word she be usin. Bernita say hey girl and I shake my head at her. Kandese got all the stuff in a duffel bag. She unzip it like she done all summer. The Blow Pops is all in a small cardboard box that used to be for her grandmuhva's medicine. Same for the taffy, the Slim Jims and the hot cheese popcorn, all sellin for a quarter more than Old Man Duney sell dem for at the general store across the tracks. Kandese had glued some nice color paper around it and wrote the prices in black marker all straight like she had dotted lines to help her. Narely, she stop her fake giggles right when the screen door opened, and now she grabbin the cartoon drawings and helpin Kandese hang dem up. Bernita, she wait for a little bit to show us she can do whatever she want and then set up the combs and scrunchies, too.

Kandese do things smart and speedy. Like she got little signs that say sale on dem and she already know where she wanna put those. She thumb-tackin dem on the porch railin and flingin her hair every once in a while to get it out the way.

That weave get longer and longer every time I see you, Bernita say.

For a second I think she talkin to Narely cuz that sure sound like a somethin-starter.

Haha, you funny Bernita, Kandese say the same way grownups

say it when they pattin you on the head. But this ain't a weave. I told you I gets it straightened.

Then she twirl like the skinny models in them magazines she be readin and I hold my smile. I wish I could snap back at Bernita fast like that, but every time she crack on my cornrows I jus freeze up.

Bernita look at me and Narely, see if we know she jus got sonned, and we pretend we still fixin up the candies on the porch. Then she put all her weight on her right foot and she ask, When we gettin our share of the money, anyway? We sold all this candy and we ain't seen near a dime, yet.

Then she look at me.

Be patient, girl, Kandese say to her. I told you I got stuff cookin. Mattafact –

She go into that duffel bag and pull out a tiny folded up sheet with an address on it. The handwritin look jus like the one on the sale signs.

This is the address to the station that be playin the news, she say. Imma write to them and they gonna do a story on us.

I'm like, Yo Kandese that's a good idea.

Even though I know personally my night is over when my mama put on the news. I jus didn't know you could send them letters cuz I didn't know they had a house. And if they had a house, I thought only white people could send letters to it.

Ain't no news cameras comin down here, Bernita say. Cops don't even come here.

She love rainin on parades.

If we write the letter, they will, Kandese say. GIRLS START BUSINESS AND MAKE MONEY. That headline is hot. News people love when people start suttin new and they the first to cover it.

Well, you write your letter, Bernita say. Jus give me my share and Imma buy me my stilettos.

Didn't I tell you Imma handle the money, Kandese say. I ain't gonna cheat nobody.

Bernita get quiet and everybody know who in charge again. The convo stop cuz some girls from down the block come thru askin for Blow Pops. Kandese say fitty cent. Narely cut on the radio. We officially open for business.

Every black girl on my block was waitin to get a look at Kandese when she first come for the summer. Her grandmuhva told us she hit a teacher with a ruler and got kicked out of her school in Harlem. I ain't even gonna front, I was sitting in the grass with the rest of the girls my age that sunny day when Miss Bristol's beat up Oldsmobile pulled down our road. I wanted to see what she lookded like. I thought she was gonna be huge like Bernita and jus as fat, seeing how Miss Bristol say her teachers was afraid of her.

I damn nearly had to clean my eyes when I saw this lil ass girl step out of Miss Bristol's car. Girl was like only three inches taller than me and I'm not even thirteen yet. She was poutin by Miss Bristol's raggedy mailbox in her capris and sunglasses and I jus kept thinkin, this is the eight grader who told the teachers to go to hell?

When she got there, everybody was jus watchin her, waitin for her to say suttin evil. She lookded like she wanted to be anywhere but here. She had some notebook under her arm and her thumbs on her cell phone busy typin a convo to somebody more important than us. So that's how those glamorous New York City girls are, I thought. I wish I had a cell phone too so I could call my girls and say things like girl wear your heels tonight, we goin out to Times Square! But, my mama would never let me have no phone. She don't even 'low me to use the cordless after a certain hour.

She ain't even look up once, I said to Narely.

Big Bernita butt in the way she do.

Bitch thinks she too good for the South, she said.

That was when she thought she could jus bully Kandese on some size shit.

But Bernita was right or at least that's what it lookded like for the first couple of weeks. She was witnessin some class-A drama and actin like it wasn't no thang. Like when Toya mom bust out the house chasin a naked dude down the street. She was runnin faster than the devil with a slipper in her hand and the dude who was twice her size was tryna run with his pants in his hands. Everybody on the block who seen it was laughin. Later on, we found out that Toya mom had came back home thirty minutes after she left cuz she forgot her factory keys and heard that baby-makin Jodeci music comin out the one room she told Toya to always keep open. Everybody was screamin for Toya mom to catch the guy. It was like the Olympics. Except for Kandese and she seen the whole thing from beginnin to end sittin on her grandmuhva porch rockin back and forth.

Same thing when the tall bitch was chasin us, which is how this whole store business started. Everybody knew we stole candy from the general store across the tracks. It wasn't even a crime no more. We must had done it so many times. Bernita would go to the front counter and talk sex to Old Man Duney. Me and Narely jus dumped Cheetos, hot popcorns, Slim Jims and strawberry shortcakes in a sack.

But the last time we stole candy from Old Man Duney, none of us knew his grown ass granddaughter was in the back room watchin us. Narely slid a whole row of hot cheese popcorns in the sack and the tall bitch came out the back with a hot comb. We was out.

Normally we put all the candy in the car on cinderblocks by Narely house, but when you bein chased and you runnin through shrubs and hedges, you ain't got time to think. Narely seen the New York City girl on her porch and said, Hold this, and we was gone.

We couldn't come outside for a while cuz it turned out that tall bitch knew our muhvas, but when we did, Bernita made us walk over with her to get the sack back. Nobody take Bernita shit or she come stompin for you. She stomped all up in Kandese grandmuhva's yard even though it was mostly weeds. I wanted to yell, Kandese, she gonna come beat you up, run inside! But I was still into frontin like I was on Bernita side back then. I shoulda known Dese had spunk cuz her porch make some loud creaks specially when you got sumo wrestlers like Bernita walkin up dem. She kept rockin in her grandmuhva chair even when the plant pots started rockin and her lemonade started swooshin.

Where the candy at? Bernita asked.

Sold it, Kandese said.

I said where's the candy? Bernita repeated louder.

Only three candy bars left. All Almond Joys. Buy it next time, Kandese said.

Bernita grabbed the sack next to the rockin chair. Jus like Kandese said there were three Almond Joys. Me and Narely looked at each other waitin for Bernita to blow up. We seen her snatch weaves, bite necks, stomp chicks out, all that. But she jus nodded and folded her arms on some who do she think she is shit. The dollar bills was layin there right next to the sack jus in case there was more questions.

Miss Bristol got diabetes. Now that Kandese here, she help out with that. Sometimes it seem like her grandmuhva forget why she got sent down in the first place, Kandese say. Her grandmuhva happy she got somebody to find the remote for her so she can watch her stories. She roll the cart for her grandmuhva when they at the market and her grandmuhva only stop when she see a member of her church group or someone she can share pumpkin pie secrets with. That sound like Miss Bristol all right, I think. Always tryna get a chore out somebody.

Today, I decide I ain't gonna wait for Bernita and Narely slow asses. Imma talk and help her set up the candy. It's one of dem really hot days and Kandese got a dirty fan stickin out of a window, but it's jus a slap in the face. I shake my head though cuz I used to look at this house as the oldest one on our block. Some people say it been there since the slavery war and I believe it. Yellow paint don't jus chip like that overnight. And it's the only house on this block that got a chimney. But this summer, it don't look old. It look like it got character and history and we addin to that history.

Kandese say she miss Harlem, but she needed to get away even though it wasn't her choice. She talkin to me like I'm her therapist and I'm noddin my head up and down, but not too fast cuz she might jus realize what she doin confessin to a little girl who ain't seen a quarter of the fast life she seen. So I'm keepin it cool but I'm lookin at her long hair and how she chew her gum all strong and confident and I'm thinkin about how many boyfriends she must got at home.

I had a hard year, she say, and I wanna ask, Why come you hit that teacher with a ruler? But instead I ask, Is you really gonna send a letter to them TV people?

She go, Yeah, but I get the feelin that Bernita ain't too fond of the idea, and I go, Bernita, Schmernita.

She laugh at me, run into the house, and come out with a piece of paper.

Read this, she say.

> Dear TV Station,
> Me and my friends got a business and we only thirteen and fourteen years old. We sell candy, combs, pitchers of famous people, CDs, scrunchies and some fruits. We poor and everybody we know is poor, but we doing something positive for the community. I beleive you should videotape us and put us on TV cause we got $396 and we aimin for $1000.
>
> Sincerely,
> Kandese Bristol-Wallace
>
> P.S.
> We all respectful girls. Kind and got manners.

Wow, I guess that's how easy it is. You can jus send a letter and get put on TV. I never really thought about how the TV people find the news, but I woulda thought it's be suttin more complicated than that. Like somebody get shot and a satellite from the moon go beep, beep, beep, and then someone at the news people house go we got some news and they jump in the van with that long microphone that they put over your head. But that don't make sense cuz Jamel got shot by the tracks two summers ago and a lot of people was standin at his funeral cuz they wasn't enough chairs and I kept expectin the news people to show up but they never did.

This is a good letter, Kandese, I say.

She say, I made sure I wrote it in my best script to let them know –

And Bernita come bubbling up the stairs with Narely and her stretched out forehead lookin like radiator rust. I freeze up, but Kandese is chillin. She hand Bernita the paper and say, Here's the first draft. Bernita read it, stay silent, and then scrunch up her face.

You spelled 'believe' wrong, she say. She only know that cuz of the song Ms Tingdale teach us.

Oh, Kandese say. She take her pen from her rocking chair and correct it. All better, she say.

Why you wastin your time writin letters anyway, Bernita ask. When the last time you seen teenagers on the news sellin candy?

She sound like a hater, but I know where she comin from. Every time we wrote letters in school, nothin happened. Ms Tingdale say if you could have dinner with anybody famous who would it be? She say write about it and we smile and put our pencil erasers on our lips and go hmmm and write a whole paragraph and she collect it. But we never get to have lunch with our person. She tell us come up with stuff to do that will make the neighborhood better and she say start the letter with 'To Whom It May Concern' and we write it and we fold it up and put it in the envelope, but Whom never write us back.

This is different, though. Kandese got a real address and a real station. Plus we got four hundred somethin dollars and countin. Them news people would be silly if they don't put us on the TV.

Any other corrections? Kandese ask and Bernita go, humph. Kandese say, I'll take that as a no.

Bernita start tappin her toe. Well, I don't care about bout TV or none a that stuff. Jus gimme my share so I could get them stilettos I seen in the window. Sides, they wouldn't want my loud ass on the news anyway. Then she start laughin like it's the funniest joke in the world.

By loud ass, she mean, fat ass. She jab Narely to force her to agree and let her know she fat too. But don't nobody call her on it. We know that got a lot to do with why she mean in the first place. Narely smile anyway, and it's a smile that say yes ma'am, but when Bernita ain't lookin, she smile another smile that say I'm not as fat as her.

Jus let me get my stilettos, Bernita go.

Then she pretend she a model goin down a runway, but she stop as soon as she realize she got earthquake steps. That's when she go where that money, anyway? All playful. Is it here, is it there? She grab Kandese bag. Is it in this?

Kandese grab Bernita hand. My eyes want to jump out and pull Kandese hand away. Don't nobody do that to Bernita and live to tell the tale. Bernita keep laughin cuz that's the only thing she can do, but Kandese is holdin her and the porch ain't creakin no more. Kandese get high and humpy shoulders and the whole situation feel like thorns gonna start poppin out of dem. I'm lookin at Kandese up and down, tryin to see if I can see the ruler girl in there and I swear I see it even if it's jus a little bit. My armpits start ticklin and I almost get scairt for Bernita. But Kandese shoulders go down again and the porch start creakin and she let go. She take the bag away from Bernita and pull out an envelope and a stamp. She lick the stamp mad slow in front of her, walk down the stairs, half a block to the nearest mailbox.

Me and Narely stand waitin for what Bernita gonna say.

She walkin around like she gonna give the South a makeover. Like she Mary Poppins and shit, bringin the hood joy, Bernita say.

Too many beats go by without nobody sayin nothin. Narely start laughin, huffin like an engine and the beats go away and Bernita happy for the moment.

L atoya come thru on Saturdays, see how her drawings sellin. Truth be told, nobody was touchin them papers with her little gods and goddesses on horses until Kandese started callin them classical art. Maya be braidin people's hair on the right side of the porch and Toya be on the left biggin up her own work. On those days, they see our shop from early in the day when the cardboard boxes still got AirHeads in dem and all the bags of chips we got is pinned up to the banisters or when Miss Bristol snatch one of us to go reach suttin for her every now and then. They see girls peek, chill, bargain over prices, talk shit and leave with bags. They see our shop when everybody leave and all that's left on the porch is hair and candy wrappers.

I don't know how Toya be showin her face so easy after her mom caught her bonin, but she do and when she get together with Bernita all they talk about is what channels they watch that they ain't posed to be watchin.

Toya stupid, though. Every cent she make off her drawings she turn around and give back to us with her Blow-Pop-fiendin self. She already bought five off the bat today. She leanin on the porch wit one a dem in her mouth and that's when Bernita come to her and say that's not how you posed to lick it. She take one of her unopened Blow Pops, take off the wrapper, push it slowly in the back of her throat and then push it out. That's how you supposed to do it, she say. Latoya go na unh, na unh then she take her Blow Pops and slide her tongue around it and go that's how. Narely watchin dem, pretendin to make sure the rest of the candy is in order.

Kandese ain't into talk like that, but it's Saturday and we make the most money on Saturday so she like whatever.

Let me get five more of those, Dese, Toya say and Kandese ring it up.

Toya grab her pops and you can tell she got more ways to show Bernita how to lick them and you can tell Bernita ain't worried about who buyin what, jus about outlickin Toya. It's hot and the sun's zappin our clothes off. It feel like every pitbull in every house on this street is barkin cuz they wanna get out the gate. It's a bad day for people with kinky hair.

Kandese go, Toya come back here and I'm thinkin finally she done had enough. Toya and Bernita look at each other like yeah maybe we did go overboard, and Toya walk over.

The money you jus gave me put us over $500, Kandese say.

Celebrate, say Toya. Celebrate, say Narely.

How, Bernita ask.

I know, Toya say and then she leave.

Wow, $500, I think. That's probably how Oprah started. We gonna be like Oprah. We gonna be store owners. Not jus one store, many stores. They all gonna have mad floors and we gonna have so much money, we not gonna sell other people's candy. We gonna have our own brand of candy and sell our own products. We gonna have mansions and Kool-Aid gonna be pourin out the faucets. Imma have a big mink coat and Imma step out limousines with big black heels and Imma call the sound that come out of them the sound of fame. So I don't care where I'm at, in a long hallway or a big ballroom, people are gonna hear the sound of fame.

My daydream go poof and I see Toya walk up Miss Bristol steps with four boys. Or should I say men. They all at least sixteen or older and got scarves tied around they heads and one of them – the leader – got three scars on his face. My heartbeat go bump, bump, bump. I look at Kandese and she already got a couple of cardboard boxes in the duffel bag and the ziplock bags with money and she zippin the whole thing. I'm expectin her to say some little joke to make it all right, but she don't say nothin and she still holdin on to the bag handle.

Congrajalashuns, the leader come up and say. I hear y'all got a successful business goin on round here.

Kandese look right past him and hold the bag tighter.

My bad, the leader say. My name is Wild One.

He put out his hand for her to shake it. His fingernails is long and I can see the grime underneath them. For the first time this summer, it look like Kandese don't know what to do. She woulda left the dude hangin, but Bernita step right in and flutter eyes at him. She got her back against the railin and arms folded around it. Her titties is bustin out of her shirt and there's spit out of the corners of her cheeks, but she lickin it away. She shake his hand and he go, This is a fine stablishmen and the boys around him say, Fa sho, That's my word, and You ain't lie. Wild One look around and then go, Who responsible for all this, and we all point to Kandese.

Wild One say, This you?

He say it so loud and shocked that his single braids bounce a little on the side of his head. He point to his temple and say, Damn girl, you must be smart.

This is suttin. This is suttin. You smart, huh?

Kandese say, Iono.

Wild One say, You frontin, you know you is.

Kandese look at him like he the three-card monte guy and she tryin not to let herself fall for the hustle.

Kandese say, Maybe.

Wild One say, Show me a report card or suttin.

Kandese say, Na.

C'mon, c'mon, Wild One say, and he look at his boys and they say, C'mon, c'mon.

Kandese look like she thinkin and finally she say okay. I'm thinkin she gonna go in the house and come back out in ten minutes, but she jus zip open the duffel bag and take out a piece a paper. It's her report card. She offer it to Wild One like it's a piece of pie 'cept she still holdin on to it and her thumb is over four of the grades. Wild One look at it with his face all concernt like he a parent and he go, a 95 in Eka, eka. He press his face closer to the paper and say, Ekanomnics, a 95 in Ekanomnics. He put his hand up to give her a high five, but Kandese let his hand stay in the air a little before she give him a soft high five back. I wanna give her a five, too, but I also wonder which one of them other classes was it where she went in on the teacher. How she get a good grade in that E class? She musta had a teacher like Ms Tingdale who make sure all the knowledge stayed in her head.

Aight, Wild One say. We takin y'all to the lake to celebrate and the boys shake they heads. They all lookin at Kandese with that nasty-man laugh. They wanna all be her boyfriend at the same time, even if they gotta let me and my mosquito bites come along too.

This don't feel right. Kandese try to come up with an excuse to say no in a way that don't get the boys mad. Store closin, I gotta bring all the stuff back in the house, she say. But the boys say, na, na, na and it's 50/50 and Kandese could win, but Bernita step in.

Oooh, she say. Where you gonna take us? Is you takin us on a date?

She push her chest so her titties is pokin out and she pull up her pants jus so the rest of her could wiggle, too. Two of the boys look at each other and whisper suttin to theyselves. Now it's five on one and I'm bout to cry cuz I ain't got enough guts to make it five on two.

Fine, Kandese say liftin her duffel bag. Let me put this away.

Na bring that wit you, Wild One say. He put his hand to his chin for a second. But there go Bernita again.

They might wanna buy some candy.

Wild One go, Yeah that's it. We might wanna buy some candy.

Kandese zip up the bag slow, waitin for someone to change they mind.

At the lake, which is past the tracks almost by where the white people live, the water look like it's boilin. Wild One sittin in the grass by the water next to Bernita and if there was a picture took of them, people would laugh at it cuz Wild One is mad teeny and he over here tryna brush his knees on big ass Bernita. They sittin in the grass pullin blades and throwin dem into the water. They gigglin and Bernita whisperin in Wild One ear, coverin her hand over his ears, tellin him secrets. She poke at Wild One zipper and he go, Stop it, stop it, but he mean the exact opposite of what he sayin.

Kandese guy whisperin in her ear. He rubbin his beard on her, but every time he try to move forward, she shake her head. Maybe she worried bout the duffel bag money, I think. She must get dudes by the swarms in Brooklyn. So she should be handlin dem better than this. There's another dude with Narely and the only interestin thing about him is waitin to see when the dude gonna realize she not that interestin.

Why did Bernita get us into this situation, I think to myself. She always gotta drag people into her trouble. Don't nobody wanna be her real friend cuz of that. She violatin every rule Mister Rogers, Barney and Officer Friendly ever taught anybody. Don't talk to strangers. Don't let people know you got money. Don't let people drag you to a place where nobody can hear you scream.

I wanna fast forward to the end of this. I wanna look at the end of the tape. Please God, tell me this turn out right. You don't know how happy I'd be if I look at the end of that tape and it show me in my bed with my 'jamas and I can fall asleep like a feather. Please show me that tape so I can see how we got out this lake.

That's when Wild One pop his head up.

See how we help y'all celebrate in style, he say.

When nobody say nothin, he say it louder, expecting yeses. We nod our heads.

And y'all the billionaires here, he say. Y'all should be takin us to the movies or the mall or suttin.

And Bernita jump up at the wrong time as usual.

I would take y'all out, she say. But we ain't even get our share of the money, yet.

He turn his eyes on Kandese like the mother in the movie do when she find out the little white girl done told a lie.

This true? he ask, ready to take back that high five he gave her at the porch.

We savin it, she say, and I can tell she annoyed that she even had to say that much.

But it's they money, too, they worked for it, he say. Wild One, the talk show host. His boys, the audience with they mmm hmmms. Bernita got her chin up at the sky like she tellin herself this is a nice sky, but she really jus happy somebody else talkin for her. Kandese don't say nothin, not cuz she disagree though. She never disagreed with Bernita in the first place. I wanna step in and be like everybody is supposed get they money, duh, but she tryna do somethin more important, stupidhead. But I can't cuz I'm jus a watcher. That's what's wrong with me. I'm jus a watcher.

So Kandese sit there silent, cuz that's all you can be when you tryin to do suttin great and you can't explain it to someone who's too caught up in the everyday to understand.

Let her get her share, Wild One say.

One of the other dudes speak up. Let her get her share, ma.

Then another one whisper, Look at her poutin. Bet she'd put that booty on you, make you work. But he whisper it loud enough for her to hear.

I gotta go, Kandese say. She let the boys know why by the way she stand up. That make Wild One stand up, too, veins runnin up his arm. They both at eye level, his eyes more redder.

Let her get her share, he say. This time it don't sound like him. It sound like the wolf he got inside him that he tryin not to let out, but he will if he got to. Before he say this, I was pretty sure everybody here knew boys was not posed to hit girls. Now I ain't so sure.

It look like Kandese ain't so sure either. Plus, there's suttin thick that's burnin the sides of everybody face, and we lettin it burn Kandese face the most. The longer Wild One stand with dem bulldog nostrils, the thicker that suttin get and back her into a corner. So Kandese jus go ahead and stop her fight. She unzip the duffel, count ten ten dollar bills out slow enough for anybody to change they mind if they wanted to. She don't know that while she countin, he countin too, and peekin in the duffel and seein the type of money he seen only if he add up all his little bits over the years. So what the wolf do? He come up with another idea.

Let Bernita hold on to the cashbox, too, he say, and Kandese is lookin at him like she's tryin to figure out is this all happenin cuz of suttin he smoked. Either way, he serious and this close away from woof-woofin. I don't think even Bernita wanted to take it that far, but she a watcher, too. Watchin Kandese hold on to the duffel bag and her dreams.

And like that Wild One, he take a step forward and take the bag away from her. Jus like that. As if Kandese wanted to give it to him in the first place and he jus helpin her out. Now, Kandese hands go from holdin somethin to holdin nothin and everybody around her go from being silent to being silenter. But what's sad in this whole thing is Wild One ain't the criminal, here. No, no, no. He jus a dude who did suttin. The criminals is us people around him, the people watchin someone shake someone else awake from a dream and not doin nothin to stop it. It make me feel so guilty that the thought in my head – and I know it's in other people's heads – is Kandese please don't say nothin else, don't say nothin that's gonna make us feel even more horrible for jus sittin there.

But she do.

We was gonna show the TV people that money, she say.

And what she say might as well float out to the lake with the air and the blades of grass we done pulled the whole afternoon. If that letter was a bird, we done already threw rocks at it until it died. Kandese turn around and walk away. Then the dudes look at me and Narely like I think y'all need to walk away, too.

I see Miss Bristol's Oldsmobile when she and Kandese gettin ready to go to the bus station. God, August always sneak up on you from behind. I jus think bout how all us girls was curious to see her when she first came thru for the summer. Now, I doubt none a them would even yawn if they found out it was her last day here.

People is funny and borin when they don't know people is watchin them. Kandese suitcase is messin up the grass cuz she had to drag it. Then again, everything else done messed up Miss Bristol grass, French fry containers and flyin newspapers. There's that broken door on the Oldsmobile that everybody know about cuz they hear Miss Bristol tryna shut it before the cock crow every mornin. There she is now tryna open the door to let Kandese get in. She gotta lift it up and push it in at the same time. She do it like five times, but the door make the same sound when you coughin out mucus and jus pop back out. Then Kandese try it, but nothin doin. All that jus make her more crouched down and sweaty.

I wonder if she think she a loser in her head. True, it was hard to

sell candy after that whole Wild One shit, but most chicks wouldn't a
bounced back like that. But I still wonder. I wonder if she feel like she
maybe gettin kicked out. She cursin anybody in her head? Is it Wild
One? Is it Bernita? I wonder if she thinkin bout that bitch, how she
didn't show her face that last month. She could have at least tell us
what she did with the money. Give us that.

I wanna run up and say, don't think you a loser, Kandese. Bernita
got hers. And while you was in the house all depressed, gossip was
flyin back to us. Gossip about Bernita and her belly. How her mother
caught her undressin and saw it and chased her with a cast iron skillet,
screamin you ain't bringin illegitimate children in the house. How she
called Wild One on the phone and he said, It could have been a whole
train of people if you know what I mean.

Miss Bristol and Kandese finally get that back door to shut. All
Kandese stuff in the back seat, so the Oldsmobile ride slower and
lower than it supposed to. I know once it ride past me, that's it. The
candy, the money, the business all done. My godmuhva cleans the
floors in the hospital and when I pull the blind up, I see her walkin up
the street. She always lookin behind her back, speedin up, to get away
from the outdoors. Like every doorstep gonna swallow her up. Like
roots gonna spring up from the concrete, grab her ankles and hold
her there forever. Even in the spring when the animals started talkin
again, everybody was racin to get to they landin. Everybody else's
landin was jus poison. That's why it was weird to see Kandese hangin
out on Miss Bristol's porch like that because until then porches was
like quicksand, the longer you was out on them, the more people saw
you dyin. But she made it different. Everybody wasn't jus goin from
work home, or summer school home. They was chillin at our store.
Even if they wasn't buy nothin, they stopped by, checked us out. I
saw guilty looks on they face. We both knew this was why they was
walkin in the first place. It was all good now. Stop by, buy some fruit,
get your hair did.

Now it's all over and I watch the Oldsmobile go slow, beggin for
somebody to pull it over.

N ow that Kandese gone, I got no choice but to be the one back to helpin Miss Bristol. I sick of her tryna get free labor out of the kids in this town. Now, I gotta tighten the plastic on the couches and make sure her diabetes medication is in that thingy that tell what day a the week to take it. Every time the phone ring, my heart jump. I want it to be Kandese. Every time I get done with a chore, I wanna take that photo album Miss Bristol got under the coffee table and see if Kandese or her mother got a picture in it or suttin. When Miss Bristol barge in, I hope she catch me and say she got more. But all she ever got for me is a fake smile and more stuff to do. Every week, I go to Miss Bristol's and she make me do all her chores and if I don't do dem all the right away, she hold her heart all dramatic and say to me, I could die any day now.

The Saturday before school start, I wait in the front room til it's reasonable enough for me to say, Miss Bristol I gotta go for the afternoon. When I do, she say, Wait. So there I am with my new school backpack, tryin not to sit my butt down too heavy on her couch so she don't tell my mom I'm disrespectful. I'm glad school startin and I can get out of this smelly-foot house. I made sure I cleaned up extra good so she won't come flaggin me back in the streets. Now I jus need the word and, deuces, I'm out.

Thirty minutes pass by and I'm like, oh hell na. So I go look for her. She in the kitchen and she obviously done forgot about me. When she finally notice me, her shoulders rumble and then stop when she see I wasn't no burglar. There's a pile of mail on her sticky table. She shuffle through it, find one. When she open it up and read it, her face go blank. After a while, she give up and hand me the envelope. I hope it's money, but then I realize I ain't seen Miss Bristol give nobody a dime in all my years of knowin her. Prolly a note for my muhva.

I look at it and it don't even got me or my muhva's name on it. Mattafact, it got Kandese's name. The address look mad official. It say suttin, suttin, suttin, television studios. Oh shit.

I wanna use tiger teeth to open it up, I slide my finger through it jus like grown-ups do when it's jus another bill they gotta pay. Then

I see the folded letter and I hold it like I shoulda washed my hands. But by now I know what it gonna say. I know it gonna say suttin like thank for your letter, we will consider your words very carefully, and continue to tune in. I already know I'm gonna read it nine hundred and ninety-nine times and that each time I read it is gonna make me sadder and by the time I get to a thousand, I'm jus gonna say, along with everybody else, that it's jus one of them letters that they send to everybody. By the five thousandth time Imma ask why come Kandese hit the teacher with that ruler and the answer ain't gonna surprise me, then Imma ask why come the news cameras ain't here yet and laugh. And by the last time I read it, I ain't even gonna be askin questions like that no more because Imma have the answers for all dem questions myself, and dem answers is gonna make me feel safe. Safe in my bubble with the rest of the Bernitas. ∎

Granta & Wesleyan

WRITERS CONFERENCE 2020

ocean vuong

amy bloom

lesley nneka arimah

kimberly burns

tayari jones

r.o. kwon

ruby rae spiegel

marilyn nelson

jason adam katzenstein

michael cunningham

robert pinsky

asiya wadud

benjamin dreyer

greg pardlo

rich cohen

sarah moon

bob bledsoe

saïd sayrafiezadeh

kirby kim

BRAND NEW.

Writers. Poets. Novelists.
Screenwriters. Showrunners. Actors. Producers.
Editors. Publishers. Agents.

Workshops. Classes. Craft talks.
Manuscript consultations.
Instruction for beginners.
Inspiration for the experienced.
Summertime. Open mic.

Ambition. Aspiration. Possibility.

June 24-28, 2020
Middletown, Connecticut, USA

FOR MORE INFORMATION AND REGISTRATION
wesleyan.edu/writersconference
writersconf@wesleyan.edu

FOLLOW US ON TWITTER
@grantawesleyan

Wesleyan University

WHY WE WALK

Ian Willms

Introduction by Adam Foulds

In 1536, Menno Simons, a Catholic priest in Friesland, concluded that Rome's doctrines were wrong and that he could not continue in that life in good faith. Like others in the growing Protestant movement, he had studied the Bible in search of the truth and found in its pages no support for the Catholic doctrines of infant baptism or transubstantiation. He joined the radical Anabaptist movement even as it was being violently suppressed by the authorities, and soon had his own following, who called themselves the Mennonites. True to their belief that Jesus taught pacifism and forgiveness, Anabaptists, including Mennonites, did not attempt to defend themselves. Deaths soon numbered in the thousands. Burnings, stonings and live burials are all commemorated in *Martyrs Mirror* of 1660, which is for many Mennonites still the most important text after the Bible. People moved great distances to find safety. Over the centuries, Mennonite communities migrated from the Netherlands to West Prussia, to the south-west Russian Empire, now Ukraine, to Canada and the United States, to South America. Russian Mennonites were persecuted under the Soviet authorities as kulaks, then as presumed collaborators with the invading Nazi forces during the Second World War. There were mass deportations to Siberia and Kazakhstan, and many perished in the Gulag. After the fall of the USSR, most of the survivors of these shattered communities left for Germany.

Ian Willms, from a Canadian Mennonite background himself, visited the places in Russia where his ancestors had lived, creating a remarkably eloquent testimony to their faithful, fugitive way of being.

The world is essentially inimical, harsh and wintry, the landscapes inhumanly large. This is the emptiness that must be traversed by the believers; these are the conditions that must be endured. We see a lone dog in the first thick flakes of a snowfall. Far away, an isolated man appears tiny as he crosses a field. The land spreads towards a distant, monotonous horizon. There is poignancy in the contrast between these vast hostile environments and the small spaces of shelter. From a distance, a settlement appears surrounded by a low boundary wall. This is community: the huddled togetherness of gathered dwellings, the deliberate, defining separation. Smoke rises from a chimney. A lit window contradicts the gloom.

There are glimmers of the reality beyond, the promise of redemption even in the darkest places. In Siberia, a line of telegraph poles stretches beside a wet road leading to a power plant built on the site of a mass grave from the 1930s. Many of the bodies buried here were Mennonites killed in Stalin's Great Terror four hundred years after their earliest ancestors died for the same convictions thousands of miles away. But can't you see, if you look, if you want to see, the crosses at the tops of the telegraph poles? And if you do find that steadfast symbol raised there, then the wires slung between the poles might speak of unbroken communication, of the Word of the Lord in continuous connection, passing from where we stand into a distance beyond our view. ∎

YENA

Che Yeun

My mother believed she would never escape our small apartment on the ground floor. We had a view of our parking spaces instead of the river that she always wanted. Whenever a car parked close to the windows, the headlights flooded our living room with a white glare. We didn't move once. Not even when her sister, who was married to a prosecutor, offered us their prized downtown unit with a river view, all for nominal rent, while she and her husband went deep into the countryside, to breathe clean air and grow peppers and reconnect with nature and reverse the course of his stomach cancer. My mother pleaded for us to accept this arrangement, but my father instructed her to refuse. He distrusted prosecutors who traded their power for wealth. That's what he said, but I knew his decision had nothing to do with justice. He needed to keep my mother far from her family, from her life before him. Soon, that prosecutor uncle had to be hospitalized after all, and so they returned to Seoul, and although my mother pleaded some more, she wasn't given the money to buy presentable clothes and ride a taxi to join her sister for the long waits at the hospital. Nor did she get the money to send a crate of ginseng essence, or a crate of rare Japanese medicinal mushrooms, or some warm cotton slippers. When my uncle finally died, my mother confessed to me her regrets. That she had agonized over wearing the right clothes and showing up in the right kind of car, when she should have been there for her sister, even if that meant taking three buses in her usual discount dresses. She should have sold our crystal cocktail glasses, which we never touched anyway, and bought something that would prove useful at the hospital, anything at all. But when it came time for the uncle's funeral, she kicked up the same dust again. She begged for new funeral clothes, it was really necessary this time, but my father reminded her bitterly that she was his wife and should get used to looking like his wife. She tried on a bunch of her old things, asking me to inspect them in sunlight with my sharp young eyes, but in the end she concluded there was nothing suitable. She skipped the funeral. All day she stayed in bed, and asked me to bring ice water, which I did, and that day the ice seemed to melt faster than ever in her glass. She apologized for making me freeze ice all day, exhausting my soft rice puppy hands, but I had to keep going because each time I refreshed her glass she sucked it all up in one breath. In the evening, the phone rang. We both knew it was my aunt. We didn't pick up. After that, my aunt never called again. And my mother never spoke of her again – of her beauty, or her luck in marriage, or the birthmark they shared, a pale blue kiss on the shoulder. That's the story of my childhood: my mother slowly surrendering hers. Maybe that was all her own doing. But it was my father who gained the most from her loss. He finally had her in total isolation, like the blankets he kicked around with his dirty sweaty feet while he played with his Game Boy until he passed out.

I fantasized about leaving home because it seemed like the kind of thing a smart child in my position would do. This child would be cold and self-serving. She would try her luck at fleeing her mother's path. She would pack a bag and run to the central market and become a stowaway in a truckload of cabbages.

Some days these fantasies felt so good that I didn't return from school until dark. Even my father noticed my lateness. What would happen if I really vanished? Would he throw her out, and order her to find me? Or would he just get rid of her too? Her weakness made me sad, and then it made me angry, and to my own surprise, it was the anger that always led me back home. That's where my anger belonged, close to hers.

As much as I wandered in the afternoons, I couldn't find enough distraction. I couldn't buy cigarettes or alcohol. I couldn't even buy movie tickets yet. But I could steal cheap earrings from the underground mall inside the train station. I never got caught. I took as many as I wanted, and sold them to classmates the very next day.

That's how I met Yena. She appeared in my classroom, wanting to buy earrings. When she walked, her uniform swished against the back of her thighs. Her bangs fell over one eye. I thought she was the prettiest girl in our school. No one else seemed to think so. She didn't have any friends.

I showed her the earrings I had left. She stroked the pink ones, long pointed spears. They were meant to look like stones, but only looked like painted plastic, which is exactly what they were. She weighed them in her palm. She parted her hair to hold the hooks against her ear, touching, or not quite. I saw both of her eyes for the first time. The plump fold of each lid.

You little bitch, she said. This shit is cheap as hell. You're going to infect my ears.

Very cheap, I responded. Even cheaper than you.

She bought them anyway, because it was an emergency. She had a date, she explained, that very afternoon. I took her three weathered bills and wished her a good time. But after the final bell of the day I saw her walking alone, on a path that didn't lead to anywhere worthy of a date, not a karaoke room, not a video-game room, not even a bakery. I followed her. She didn't stop until she reached a phone booth. She went inside, picked up the receiver, but didn't punch any numbers on the dial pad. After a few seconds, she began to talk. Her hands, her feet, her slinky bangs, her new dangling earrings: every part of her seemed animated by an urgent conversation. But she hadn't fed any money into the phone.

The longer I watched, the more I liked her. And the more I liked her strange performance. When had it begun, talking into a phone by herself? Did she imagine a real person on the other end? Was it the same person every time? Did she give this person a name, a body, a family? Was she in love? And what were the earrings for? Did she even want them? Or had she given me money just to talk to me?

By the time she hung up and stepped out of the booth, and wiped her hands on her uniform blazer, and tossed her new ugly earrings into a trash bin, I knew we would grow close. Close, the way any two girls around here grow close, because there isn't much else to do, and anyone who makes you forget how little there is to do, anyone who makes your heart race, is someone you suddenly cannot live without.

How was your date, you slut? I asked her the next day.

Terrible, she said. He got shit-faced and kept trying to drag me to a love hotel.

Did you go?

Yeah, I just needed the money.

How much?

What?

How much money did he give you?

She paused. I don't know, she stammered. I spent it all.

The next time I saw her in the phone booth, I pressed my palm into the greasy glass door. She hung up and stepped outside.

Did you follow me here? Like a creepy whore?

Yeah.

Are you in love with me?

Want me to give you real money?

But Yena didn't want cash. She wanted cans of hairspray and computer cleaner spray. She showed me how to huff them at the riverside. After a few cans, we bought cartons of coffee milk, strawberry milk, banana milk to soothe our coughs. We sat on dry grass. To watch a Seoul sunset, just some smog, scattered light in cream. The brown river lapped away with all kinds of trash, municipal signboards and bicycle seats.

We drifted under one of the seventeen bridges of our city, counted pigeons, huddled in the nooks, shivering, sleeping. We threw stones at them and watched them flee in panic. They beat their wings into thunder. We laughed. We began with pebbles but soon we hurled chunks of brick. We said it was the cans of fumes fucking us up, but we knew it wasn't. The pigeons always came back. No matter how hard we threw, how often.

When the sprays hit us a little too hard, we dozed off by the levees. We learned to sleep outside without fear. We learned to sit with legs wide open. We learned how much we needed these small steps, that they felt colossal next to nothing.

Our arms and legs grew dark in the sun. We would wake up when cops came by, yelling at us to go home. Or when someone threw crap at us, like the older girls from our school, or passing cyclists. We cussed out the older girls. We cussed out the cyclists, too.

We cussed out our teachers. We cussed out botany, which we never understood because we had to learn it in a forgotten garden at the back of our school grounds.

And then we began to smoke with the older girls in the garden. We watched, as the older girls discarded their cigarette butts into a pile the size of a rat. They spat on the weeds. It didn't matter how often they got caught and lashed for smoking. Or for skipping class. Or for talking out of turn. Or for reading comic books. Or for wearing makeup, for dyed hair, permed hair, any hair that extended more than three centimeters below the ears. They simply took their lashings in the front of the classroom. Sometimes they took them in the middle of the soccer field, so that every student in the building was forced to watch. The loud cracks echoed off the brick walls. Our teachers threatened them with more violence, expulsion and stories of fallen women they had witnessed over their careers.

Think you're the first to feel invincible? They yelled while they beat the girls with wet towels and kendo swords. Aren't you afraid of the sky? Think you're the first to get beaten like this and never learn?

Yena never stole anything with me. Instead, she waited outside. She wore a backpack that looked exactly like mine. As soon as I exited the shop, we traded bags and walked fast without looking back. That way, even if the shopkeeper noticed me, or saw me on security footage, and chased me down, he would only find Yena's things, her lip gloss, her face powder, her aerosols. But I never got stopped. Each time, the shopkeeper received my smile with the same nod. *You dick,* I thought, *how does a slow sad dick like you get by?*

We cut our hair in the school bathroom, trimming the ends to a perfect straight edge. The older girls laughed at us, but soon they asked to borrow our scissors. They worked with quiet concentration, to the thick sound of blunt blades scraping together. It spread like a disease, the pleasure of beautifying each other.

At the last minute, Yena grabbed the front of my hair and lopped off whatever didn't fit into her fist. Now I had bangs too. She trimmed and shaped it into a leaf over my right eye.

What are you doing?

I'm giving you my look. Our look. Now no one else can have it.

I examined myself in the mirror. My right eye was gone, buried. Only my left eye remained to take in the entirety of the world. It looked bigger on its own. Bigger, and even brave. I thought of my mother, and the sister she no longer saw. I had always taken after both of them. Even my father had commented on our likeness. But now, with only half of my face on display, the resemblance was also halved. I thought I looked smarter than either of them, with my own slimy secret tucked under my hair. I decided I would keep this look, our look, for the rest of my life.

Some of the older girls tried to discourage me from continuing my friendship with Yena.

We know you love her, they said in between their endless puffs in the garden. And we feel a little shitty maybe for what we're about to say. But basically it's this. She's not someone you want to take care of.

So?

So stop it. She's pretty but that just hides the problem.

And what's her problem? I asked. I heard a wavering in my voice I didn't recognize. I tried to swallow it, but it wouldn't budge. What problem is she hiding?

Look she's creepy as shit and it's not okay. She doesn't look right. She doesn't talk right. She lies. She's untethered. She's rotting inside. And if you take all those things they add up into a big fucking problem. She's the kind of girl who's going to snap one day. The kind of girl they make all those psycho schoolgirl horror movies about. You're not listening to any of this, are you? You don't see it? At all?

Well there's plenty wrong with me too, I said. And with all of us.

But one afternoon, I woke up on the bank of the river, alone, surrounded by our used and unused cans. I called out for Yena, but she didn't answer. Had she stumbled home? The afternoon traffic remained quiet and easy on the bridge. It couldn't have been that long. She had to be somewhere close by.

I found her in the phone booth. She wasn't talking into the receiver. She was just curled up on the floor of the booth, leaning against the glass. I banged on the door with a fist.

Get up you dirtbag.

She looked up. You need to help me, she said.

She moved her legs so I could join her inside. She raised her arms to show me a pigeon tucked behind her, into a grimy corner of the booth. There was a gash on its head.

I did this, she confessed. I'm a cruel piece of shit.

I pulled her up, and she stepped outside of the booth to keep watch. I knelt by the pigeon to examine its condition. I looked into its wet red eyes. When I leaned closer, an odd smell made me recoil.

Hey, we heard someone shout from the footpath. He looked like somebody's father. He was dressed in a helmet and cycling spandex but we didn't see a bike.

Hey, you girls okay? What's going on here?

We ignored him and he slunk away again.

What's wrong with me? Yena asked. Why did I do this?

I tried to reassure her. Come on. We throw shit at them all the time. Everyone does.

She squinted up at the gray clouds.

Dogs, she said. They'll eat it up, won't they? They'll go nuts. Let's put it in the river.

She was afraid to touch it by herself, so we did it together. We rolled the pigeon into the open face of my geography textbook. I touched its head, a warm acorn. I couldn't tell if it was breathing anymore. We carried the book to the river and released it onto the waves like a barge. The book sank almost immediately, but the bird floated away, swept up by the current. I watched it become the size of a fist, then a finger, then a fingernail, until it disappeared.

Why did I do that? Yena asked again.

Don't worry about it, I said. I reminded her of how dirty this river already was. From all the crap we kicked into it. Broken bottles, leftover noodles and, according to the news, the occasional human life heaved over the edge in despair. In comparison, a bird seemed clean and uncomplicated. We washed our hands at the fountain and walked home.

Before we parted, I gave her my uniform blazer so that I could take her bloodstained one. It was a barely noticeable mark, it even looked ornamental, like a stamp, but I wanted Yena to forget today as quickly as possible. We squeezed into each other's clothes. She finally broke into a smile.

You're never getting this back, she said. Yours is so much warmer.

They're the exact same.

Yeah but you take good care of yours. You know how to make this last. Not another useless cunt after all.

That night, when the apartment fell quiet, I took Yena's blazer into the bathroom. Once I unfolded it, alone, I noticed all kinds of stains and spills on the fabric. Today's blood would come out easy. But the other stains looked deep. It looked like she hadn't washed it since the beginning of the school year.

I filled the bathtub with cold water. I submerged the blazer, then rolled up my pajama legs to stand in the tub. I stepped on it. Left, right, together, right, left, together, the way my mother stepped on mine, while she kept my underwear boiling in a pot on the stove.

The splashes woke my mother. She tried the knob on the door.

What are you doing in there?

I'm washing my feet, I said.

Is the water warm?

Yeah.

Can I wash them for you?

It's okay. Just go back to sleep.

Let me see your little feet. I haven't seen them in such a long time.

I'll show you later.

I waited for her to return to bed before carrying the dripping blazer back to my room. I flipped it inside out, and then I ironed it, over and over, until the hiss of steam went away.

Oh my God, Yena exclaimed when I brought her blazer to school. She scrunched the fabric into her face and took a deep breath. It smells better than the day I bought it. She shoved the fabric into my face as well. You are so totally in love with me aren't you?

I just want my blazer back?

She helped my arms into the sleeves. It felt looser in the shoulders, and around the waist. I wondered if she had worn it to bed, tossing around all night, stretching it out. I looked for other changes. There was a new stain on the front pocket. It could have been mascara, breakfast, a mosquito squashed in her sleep. It could have been anything, but I didn't mind. Don't ever wash it off, don't even touch it, I promised myself.

When it got too cold to huff by the river, Yena came over. For once I was ecstatic about our ground-floor apartment, because all I had to do was slide my window open to let her climb inside.

I wanted to hide her in my room, but she was determined to meet my mother.

You have a nice mother, she explained. I've never lived with a nice mother before. I want to see what it's like.

My mother cut up a pear and an apple, fanning the slices on a plate. She brought out cups of grape juice, and then she sat with us and asked Yena about her family, her schoolwork, what she wanted to be when she grew up.

Anything, was her answer. I just don't want to be a housewife. Boredom is poison.

My mother was hurt, but she hid it well. Of course, she said. Your generation, you have so many possibilities now.

What would you do? Yena asked her. If you could do it again?

I think I'd be right here, with you girls.

What if you didn't have girls? If you had boys instead?

I guess I'd be running around, cleaning up their mess.

Your back would break like fuck from all that cleaning.

My mother laughed. Yes it would. That's why I said I'd rather be right here with you.

When we had the apartment to ourselves, Yena poked through my mother's clothes. Nice mother clothes, she called them. She finished with the shabby dresses and went to the bathroom, where all our bottles of makeup and cream were squeezed to the very last squirt and disposable plastic gloves were hanging up to dry. She went through the kitchen, and held up the bottle of washing-up liquid, formerly a deep blue, now colorless, because we had diluted it with water over and over again.

Dogs, Yena said. You remind me of dogs licking an empty bowl forever.

I got angry. Stop looking, I said.

Okay fine. I'm sorry.

You're still looking.

I'm sorry, okay? I can't help it.

How about next time we go look at your stupid dog-bowl life?

Ha. Yena spat into the sink. You wouldn't know what to do with my dog-bowl life. You wouldn't last a day.

I stared at her saliva. I thought about saving it, the way I had saved her stain on my blazer, and the dirty old bills she had given me. I could scoop up her spit and freeze it into a cube. I could keep it to remind me of how much we needed each other. But all of a sudden, I didn't want to be reminded of that anymore. Was it true that I wouldn't last a day in her life? How would a day of hers even begin? I didn't know. She was essentially a stranger. And yet I had invited her into my home. And now I was fantasizing about enshrining her spit in ice, all in order to feel close to her. I hated how stupid I had revealed myself to be, how stupid my loneliness had made me.

I ran the tap and let it flush the sink. We flopped onto my bed. We shared a pillow and split a can, and then we blinked our eyes. Yena's pupils dilated into wormholes. We split another can, sucked on ice cubes, and finally calmed down. When we ran out of cans we looked for something else to sniff. We unwrapped the soap I had swiped before, a round bun that promised purple flowers from France. We felt silly holding it, but at least we had something nice to smell.

Just so you know, she slurred. You're going to end up like this. Like her. Like your slave.

She's not my slave. She's my father's slave. He's the asshole.

But you're the one she endures him for. She's sticking around for you. You're the one she's trying to save. And it's not going to work.

We dozed and drifted. When she got out of bed and picked up her shoes and climbed out of my window, I pretended I was still asleep.

The next time I passed a convenience store, I went inside and bought a bottle of washing-up liquid. The cashier didn't look up. I knew I could have stolen it, but this time it felt better to pay. At home, I mixed it with the old watery bottle. It was much harder than I thought, blending two full bottles of liquid together, pouring one into the other, back and forth, and then shaking them, and then waiting for the foam to settle until they finally became equal.

When my mother came back, I showed her what I'd done. She was so delighted that she rushed out to treat me with fried chicken for dinner. She watched as I ate the pieces, stripping them down, leaving nothing to waste, not even cartilage. She lifted my bangs to rub her palms all over my oiled face.

Are you my slave? I asked her.

Do you want me to be?

No.

Then I'm not.

We saved the pickles in cling film and sprawled out in the living room until my father came home. He parked his car hurriedly, facing our unit. But he didn't come out. The headlights stayed on, and for a while all we could see was the harsh light. But then our eyes adjusted, and we made out the streaks of rain on the windows. Soon we could see into the car, where my father remained in the driver's seat, engrossed in his Game Boy, hunched over to finish some squeaky game.

I felt, for the first time, that I would never run away. I would stay right here after all, close to my mother. I would hold on to her until she was empty, like a spray can or a cigarette. By then I might have my own husband, who would try to use me up. I could sense who my husband might be, the kind of man I avoided on the bus, eyes bleary from video games and alcohol.

I lifted my arm. It fell on my mother. Her eyes were closed, because it made her sad to see my father spellbound by his device. I dropped my arm on her again.

Mmm, she said.

I'm going to have a pretty disgusting ordinary life, I revealed to her.

It's not so bad, she said. I'm not so bad. Compared to so many of my classmates. So many girls I lost touch with. I think about them all the time. They would be so happy to have my life right now. I hope they're okay.

What if they're not okay?

Mmm?

What if you have a friend who is not okay? Right now? What do you do?

I don't know, daughter. Maybe you help them. Maybe you drift apart. It's hard enough to keep one person afloat. One person still floating anywhere is a miracle. And they know that too. So maybe they understand.

I wondered if she was thinking about her sister, who might be all alone now, in her downtown unit, or maybe her daughter was with her, pressing her face into her neck. When my mother fell asleep, I listened to her snores. I tried to smell her heart through her chest. It was something I had always tried to do. I was convinced I would smell it there one day, a cool mass the color of her tongue. Then my father walked in.

Hey. He nudged her with his foot. Hey. Wash before you sleep.

She washed already, I lied.

Bullshit. I could smell her from the parking lot.

I bundled her in my father's blankets, even though I knew he would pull them away from her. He required all the space of the living-room floor, the warmest spot in the flat. I waited for him to fall asleep too. I wanted to smell his heart, which I had never tried before. I looked at his chest, and the hairs swirling into a dark cloud. I hovered closer. One degree at a time. I held my breath so it wouldn't tickle him. I didn't want him to open his eyes and see how close we were becoming. How close I was to his secrets. No one had ever gotten this close. Not my mother, not even his mother, because they already knew what I sensed right now: that even as he slept his heart never stopped watching us. I breathed in. There it was. Loud. Slippery. Unforgiving. And it wanted to outlive me. I knew this would likely never be the case, that any reasonable person would bet that I would outlive him. I was already outliving him, I just didn't know it yet. But his heart didn't care. It wasn't finished growing, and I smelled how much bigger his heart wanted to become. It promised me we would never be done.

I couldn't sell cheap earrings for the rest of my life. If I wanted money, real money, to get a new dress for my mother, and a gift-wrapped crate of sweet pomegranate essence, and then call a taxi for her to carry the crate with ease and elegance to her sister at her river-view flat, where they could reconcile, and order fried chicken and some beer, and hold each other in the blue glow of the most dazzling bridge in our city, I would need a lot more. I would need a job.

I interviewed at every convenience store in the neighborhood, but they wanted a boy, tall and strong enough to intimidate shoplifters and carry large boxes. I even approached the shopkeeper I'd stolen from all year. But he couldn't hire anyone because the shop was folding. The rent was tripling. He confessed he needed a job himself, and the conversation ended with him asking me a favor instead, I was to find out through my parents and my neighbors if anyone worked in an office building or a school or a mall in need of a new security guard. I promised I'd ask everyone, but I didn't.

At the end of the month, the shop closed and got replaced by a dress store, and the young woman who ran it tried her best to elevate the cramped space with a chandelier and delicate wallpaper.

My classmates were changing, too. They were getting serious about university. Serious about exams, cram schools, boyfriends, husbands, skincare, haircare, dental care. They were trickling into school with new eyes and new noses, sometimes still wrapped in thick bandages. They were acquiring taste. Their Prada backpacks didn't match their old cheap earrings. From now on they needed yellow-gold hoops, or rose gold, or white gold, or small diamond studs.

When my mother offered to send me to cram school, I told her to save the money. I convinced her I'd top the rankings on my own.

I stopped seeing Yena. We barely went to the river, even after the ice melted. When we passed out, I woke up before she did. I abandoned her on the riverbank. It didn't feel good, leaving her unconscious body on a slab of concrete, but at least there was no one to see me do it.

Afterwards, I told her I'd gotten too fucked up, that I'd stumbled home.

Are you falling out of love with me?

She wasn't really joking.

What if we get raped out here? I asked in return. And then they just roll us into the water?

I pinned my bangs away from my face, and waited for them to grow out.

When Yena tapped on my window, I didn't get up to let her in. I stayed put at my desk with my stack of homework. She jiggled the stiff frame, but I had already locked it a long time ago.

I'm busy, I mouthed to her. We could have easily heard each other through the thin glass. I didn't want us to.

You're not busy, she mouthed back at me. You're not doing shit.

Yena stayed at the window, daring me to look away. Her skin had darkened from the long afternoons by the river, even though it was barely spring. I wondered how she kept warm. She licked her lips, chapped from dry sandy winds. Her bangs were caught in the gust too, her tattered flag, flapping and pointing every which way. The skin between her eyes showed, the most beautiful part of her body, but this time I did not want to touch it at all. She looked back at me, but also at my bed, my desk, my reading light, my new awards framed on the wall, for debating and sewing. Soon I would also win awards for poetry and English and paper-boat-making. I was learning that there was nothing I couldn't accomplish. It was easy, now that I lived with the shiny purpose of one day saving my mother so that she could stop saving me. I had almost let Yena come between us, but not anymore. Now I had a reason to breathe in each gulp of air. Not even Yena could laugh at me. It might even make her cry. I wanted to make her cry, for thinking she could ever be family, for thinking she could ever pull me into her burrow.

Look away, I mouthed at her. And she did.

Maybe that should have been it. Maybe that's when we should have drifted apart. But after a long day of boring classes, I went to the school garden to smoke with the older girls. They were pressed together, nursing the ear of a girl who had been caught with her gold-plated hoops in the middle of class. The teacher had smacked her head around, and then she'd pulled one hoop right out. It tore through the lobe, and now the girl was bleeding, and she was also never going to get her eighty thousand won back, and we took turns pressing a water bottle to her bandaged ear, and we were weighing how best to take revenge on the pathetic cunt who would do this to a child, how to take pictures and file a complaint with the police, or maybe just follow the teacher home and corner her in an alley and let our instincts take over.

As we smoked and plotted, a girl lifted her shoe. She bent over to study the stale hardened soil, and then she dug her toe deep, until she kicked up something.

What is this?

We dug together, with all of our toes, until we unearthed a pigeon. It was very dry, and very dead, we knew right away, but we stepped back, in case it took flight. We tossed an old pack of gum, just to see it land on the limp neck.

Who did this? What psycho fuck did this? What chicken testicle fuck is fucking with us?

Before I could stop myself, I said, Yena.

I clasped my hands over my mouth. I knew that wasn't true. I knew Yena would never do this, that she would never pollute or intrude upon my new life, because in some unthinkable way, she still needed me. Don't lie don't lie don't lie, I thought to myself. But then I also thought, don't be so sure. Don't kid yourself. Don't wait. So I dropped my hands.

It's her, I said. And there was another one before. An even smaller one.

It didn't take long for the older girls to decide what to do. Even the one with the torn ear, the one who was headed for the police station, agreed to join this operation instead. I took them to the tunnel that led to the bike path and the reed bushes by our spot on the river. Yena was alone. When she saw us, she got up. The older girls pulled her back down. We pulled her by her hair, by the collar of her blazer, by her shoes. When she kicked them off, we grabbed her ankles. You little cunt. You murdering shitbag. We crammed dirt into our fists, and pushed it into her eyes. We pushed it into her nose. We pushed it down her throat. No one could stop us. Not Yena, who only curled her head down to her stomach, trying to slow her blood. Not the cyclists, who braked into a sudden crowd, craning, yelling. No one is worth it, they shouted at us. No one. ∎

Queer Pan-African Joy as Revolution: A Portrait of Binyavanga Wainaina, 2017

BINYAVANGA

Pwaangulongii Dauod

It is now a matter of acceleration. The energy is active, mobile, he said. It is time for kinetic existence. I am reading his notes about ships in high transits, submarines, spaceships, nuclear energy. The exorcism has long ended.

'Hey Binyavanga, what's the noise about?'

It is a question thrown at him by someone from the house next door. It is a dark house and the person is invisible to us when we turn around to take a look.

'Let us go,' Binyavanga says. I am reluctant. 'Boy,' he says, 'quit waiting for that voice. Quit waiting for that motherfucker hiding in the darkness. It is now a matter of acceleration.'

Let's go.

We are in a neighbourhood near the government quarters in Kaduna, where Binyavanga is *building* a large workspace. It will be a place for creative people: offices, rooms, studios, computers, internet, bookshop and a library. It will be an *open space*, the happiest and most creative and liberal workplace in the world. From here, he said one recent night while standing in the middle of the compound, we will curate the Open Space Festival, a literary Glastonbury, and stir a new school of imagination across the continent. Next year we will begin work on a large farm. We are setting up a restaurant in town, opposite the state university. Later this year, maybe in October, we will travel through Central Africa: a journey that will end in Senegal for a sci-fi workshop.

'Let's go,' Binyavanga shouts. I am reluctant but my feet quicken; something is moving, crawling in my body.

Days later he and I stand on an old mossy embankment facing the Kaduna River. Two shirtless fishermen are paddling past us; a boy of ten or eleven sits in the front of the boat smoking a cigarette with one hand and grabbing the fishing net in the water with the other. The water is neither clean nor dirty. It's a little transparent, so that the rocks beneath the surface show. The scene is a verse from the poetry of Derek Walcott; the poetry of fish, the poetry of water immersing Golgotha.

We are in Kaduna metropolis. So dreamy. The past days have been trafficked in energy. Now everything is calm, an exhilarated aura descends on us. '*Je suis calme*,' Binyavanga says. We are still standing on the embankment. He turns to face me and makes a sweet face. His face glistens in the evening air. There is a taste of water in the air. '*Je suis calme*,' he says again, and this time he pouts, femininity spilling over his face. I feel so happy. His voice is rich with coffee. In the past this voice has been filled with beer and cigarettes – these, and love.

He moves away from me and steps down on to the concrete. On land he puts his right foot into the soil like a herbalist, the way my grandmother did in the fields, and toes out some earth. What does it smell like? Burnt farmland? The legacy of ancient fire? Or does it smell of the wind? Asking these questions with a sudden intensity, Binyavanga seems to be in a trance. As a child, he says, he once dreamed of being a tornado, a whirlwind, something forceful and mobile, or, in better words, something forcefully mobile. 'I possessed an affinity with chaos. That's why I came to trust language.' He says he would stand in the back of his father's pickup or tractor on some field in Nakuru, in the Kenyan Rift Valley, hands spread wide against the passing wind. He loves air, clean air, fire and water, he says: these are the elements that make up a free man. He moves further down the river and scoops more soil, this time with his left hand. What does it smell like? Dead fish? It smells like water?

I collect a handful of the soil and smell it. 'Binya,' I say, 'it smells of deadness. The place smells of dead leaves, leaves that have stopped being lush and have come to new ashen colors of grey, brown and earthy poetry.'

'Quit being sentimental,' he says. The man detests sentimentality and melodrama. He desires to simply arrive at naked meaning. Whatever is stripped bare. Perhaps this is his reason for walking back to meet me where I stand on the embankment. His walk has transitioned to a sashay, so appealing when I allow myself to see the movement of the tutu he is wearing around his waist. He is a big man, a man who has become my second mother.

He removes his shirt, and dives into the night river. Two strokes. Four strokes. Eighteen strokes and he is in the middle of the river, a river full of crocodiles and tilapia and fresh water. Binya. Binya. Binya. Binyavangaaaa. My dry throat tries to crack. I cup hands around my mouth. 'Binya. Binya. What is your destination? Where are you swimming to?' He hears me. He laughs a big laugh that shakes the four corners of the water. 'Me,' he says, 'I can swim anywhere and anytime I like. Me, I am a free man.' Another laugh. 'Me,' he says, 'I have always dreamed of freedom. Where am I swimming to? To Africa. To Africa. On my way back I will bring my mom with me.'

'Binya, are you bringing back your baba too?'

'Yes,' he says, 'I am bringing them back to Kenya. I will also bring more imagination.' Two strokes. Four strokes.

I cup my hands around my mouth one more time and shout. 'Does the river go all the way to downtown Nairobi?'

'Yes. Yes. I think so,' he answers. 'And if it does not, I will link it there. Water or air, Kaduna to Nairobi is a four-minute flight. Binyavanga Airways. Flight: 18/01/1971–2019.'

Daydreaming is a form of prophesying, too.
In one of Binyavanga's writing classes in New York, he refused to accept dreams in his students' writing because, he said, it's so melodramatic. Writing, or literature, he argued, gesturing with his hands in the air, is already in itself enough dream.

I am disobeying him. I will have dreams in my sleep, and I will write them in literature. Did he not once tell me that he would break any rule that was unappealing to his imagination?

On June 29, 2016, Binyavanga Wainaina summoned me to his hotel room in Lagos to say that he was thinking of visiting Kaduna. He was teaching a writing workshop alongside his longtime friend, Chimamanda Adichie, and I had just arrived from Kaduna three days earlier to spend time with him. Since 2007 Binyavanga had been visiting Nigeria every year to teach workshops or attend literary festivals. 'Lagos,' he once told me, 'is the one city in the world where I find everything to be complete. It is unpretentious and ultimately postcolonial. I love being in postcolonial spaces.'

Binyavanga had suffered a series of strokes in 2015 and, even though we stayed in close touch via email and telephone, this was our first meeting in nearly a year. That June morning, I went to his hotel room and found him at a table hunched over tea and his MacBook Pro. His head was shaved, except for a small, thin patch of hair that was dyed blue. He wore a white bathrobe, and there was a hint of coffee in the room. The strokes had affected his tongue; his speech was slurred. He was writing two 'big books about the continent', and planned to visit places that would expand his vision of Africa: Zaria, Kaduna, Kano, Nok, Timbuktu, the Nuba Mountains, Bangui. The trip to Kaduna, he said, would be an opportunity to go to Lokoja and stand at the bank of the Niger Benue confluence, as well as to visit my mother. He hadn't met her (and would not meet her), but he had sent money several times to help cover the medical expenses for her chronic illness.

July 2 2016, we took a flight from Lagos to Kaduna. Binyavanga was too ill to continue to the hotel. He was dehydrated, and fainted in my arms just as we disembarked from the plane. We waited at Kaduna Airport for some two hours. Immense fatigue had seized his body. He refused to go to the hospital for rehydration, drinking several bottles of soda water instead. Twice he vomited uncontrollably. I sat beside him, holding him. It was obvious that he was too sick for this journey. Another person would have postponed the trip, but not Binyavanga. Even against nature, he sought freedom.

His cough was dry and sickly. He sat in a chair in the waiting area sweating, staring at me and at everything, an empty look that obviously stemmed from suffering. When he spoke, his speech slurred and childish, it was to ask about the book I was writing. And, curiously, he talked about death in a visceral sense. Since we had met up a few days earlier he had become mildly but seriously obsessed with his own mortality. It was the beginning of pessimism in Binyavanga. 'I wake up these days thinking I won't finish the books after all,' he told me that evening at Kaduna Airport.

That was my first time with Binyavanga in a low moment. He was travelling on a slim budget, utterly dependent on my presence. I knew the pin code to his bank card, and read his emails to him. For the first time, someone I so adored and loved for his force, for his independence and strength, appeared vulnerable.

There must be ways to organise the world with language. As hopeless as everything might appear, the simple arrangement of words can tame chaos.

But Binyavanga had a temperament that thrives in chaos. He had just resigned from his teaching job at Bard College, an attractive position.

In the weeks before Binyavanga dived into the River Kaduna, where he promised to return with his father and mother and imagination, before he declared '*Je suis calme*', my life had become chaotic. I was without language, and had no way to tame the violence of distance. Binyavanga had not been replying to my emails. The chaos accelerated when my emails failed to reach him, because his inbox was full. February 15, 2019, he had emailed to say that he loved and missed me, that he was recovering from another stroke, that he was in a serious but stable condition.

May 11, 2019, I discovered that Binyavanga had suffered another series of seizures and strokes and had been placed in intensive care. My desire to travel to Kenya and visit him deepened. His sister Ciru told me he was in a coma. Someone else said he'd had difficulty seeing for a time.

Use language to tame chaos.

It was in an apartment in Dakar. This was January 2011. Binyavanga was still teaching at Bard. A little party was happening that night. An after-party. He had given a talk on the writing of Alain Mabanckou earlier that evening. Five people were dancing. A big woman with her hair dyed blond walked over to meet Binyavanga. 'Happy birthday,' she said, and led him to the middle of the room, surrounded by the other slowly dancing people. Binyavanga's hair was dyed yellow and blue. His jacket, made of Senegalese fabrics, was light yellow and sky blue, embroidered with leaves and trees. He wore a pair of silvery sneakers, and they shone in the low light of the room. His trousers were black, and if one looked closely they seemed to sag at the waist.

The woman was leading the dance, but Binyavanga was involved too. He looked the woman in the eye, his right hand held her left and his left hand stayed on her waist; they looked like lovers making up for lost time after a quarrel. I stood by the door, smoking a joint, passively relishing the party.

'Where is Igoni Barrett?' he asked. 'Is he not coming to the party too? Remember that from here I'll be going into a coma. Remember.'

Coma is the place for gathering momentum. Thereafter, the acceleration. Why does Wangechi Mutu wonder why butterflies leave powder on the fingers? It is only a matter of acceleration.

July 2, 2016. By the time Binyavanga had checked into his hotel room in Kaduna, nearly four hours after we left the airport, he had passed out twice. A doctor recommended that I stay close and watch him all night. He was supposed to give a late-night interview to a journalist from Abuja, and I cancelled the appointment without informing Binyavanga. I was now effectively combining the roles of friend, guide and caregiver. He got into bed and I took another room.

Two a.m., I went to check on him. The light was on. Opening the door, I found Binyavanga awake, sitting at the table with his computer. The AC was on high; the room was cold. He said he was fine. He couldn't sleep, but his strength had returned. He said he wanted moi-moi. I moved to the bedside and used the telephone. It was too late to prepare moi-moi, the kitchen said. He said he would like anything that was peppery. Hot chicken wings. Hot spaghetti. Chicken wings were possible.

'Which of the young writers in Kaduna do you think deserves representation, an agent?' he asked, turning from the computer to face me. His intention was clear enough and his strength was visible, but his slurred speech invoked pity. I had learned to listen to him without showing a reaction.

'Writers who you think need agents,' he emphasised.

Hajara Hussaini Ashara. We were friends. Schoolmates in Zaria. Katung Kwasu. We are friends. He was my first true reader.

'Get me their works. I have to read them before daybreak.'

I emailed him a book-length manuscript by Hajara and a short story by Katung.

The wings arrived. Binyavanga wanted to have them with soda water.

He refused to go back to bed all night. To a fault, Binyavanga put other people's progress above his own. You could argue that his writing slowed down because he was preoccupied with establishing other writers, as well as a publishing house. There are many writers, including myself, who owe their careers to Binyavanga. He was the most generous writer of his generation.

Binyavanga, I believe, saw himself as a link between privilege and generosity. He desired Power (capital P) because it was the only way to bring the revolutions he nursed in his mind to reality. He believed he was a member of the group, or the platform, that had to take charge of the African continent. He began building a movement across Africa and the black world that he named Upright People. When talking about this, Binyavanga found expression in the following words: Sankara, love, middle class, African languages. There was a socialist sensibility to his thinking. His essays should not appear behind paywalls; writing would be a collaborative effort between African curators, writers and translators; businesses would be set up and run by the community. He had gone on a forgiveness spree of his 'enemies' in the literary space on the continent. 'Boy,' he said. 'Everyone has to come on board. No more time for hate.'

Several days after we arrived in Kaduna, my friend Katung suggested a tour of the library: a small room with high, white walls and bookshelves. Katung and I had both worked there as volunteers in 2015.

The two men walked away from the crowd on the lawn and climbed up the stairs to the library. I moved closer to the building. I had noticed that Binyavanga was sweating, and I had his soda water.

Inside the library, Binyavanga moved around the shelves, head to one side, gleaning the titles, when suddenly he turned and hurried out. Katung followed him. Binyavanga was crying.

What had happened?

All eyes were on him.

'How dare you,' Binyavanga cried. He was not addressing anyone in particular. 'This is the whitest library in the world. How dare you. You cannot even find anything close to this in England or America.' He was weeping now. 'A library in Africa that does not have books by Chimamanda, Helon or me? How dare you.'

He walked out of the compound. 'Take me out of here,' he said, in-between sobs. 'I will never give a reading in such a terrifying place. Take me somewhere else.'

Baby sister Ciru and Binyavanga were playing in the yard. Ciru sat in the sand; around her were some balls of blue yarn and knitting needles. It was Binyavanga's thirteenth birthday and for some reason he had asked for blue butterflies. Since his seventh birthday he had been obsessed with butterflies. Butterflies and books. He dreamed about both the way you dream about pleasure. His head was full of colours and words; two vital parts of language. Even as a child he knew that chaos could only be tamed by language. An unknown imagination had begun invading his system. 'This is why,' Binyavanga once said, 'I am still possessed by the Nandi woman; the woman standing on the wall of the kitchen.' Ciru was knitting the gifts: handcrafts. Binyavanga was inside the house looking at the painting of the Nandi woman. As a matter of fact, he wanted the butterflies from Ciru so that he could put them around the painting.

'Hi, Ciru. Is Binyavanga recovering well?'

'Yes; but he's still in a coma.'

'I am thinking of him. I love him so much.'

'Thank you. We all should continue to love and pray for him.'

Little Ciru's arms were fatigued. Four hundred butterflies had been created. Blue butterflies. Binyavanga had been out there with her but was just summoned inside by his mom. His dad lay on a couch in the living room reading an English magazine; he was keen on articles about tea. An Englishman had written an interesting take on growing tea in East Africa. Not about marketing and distribution and export. Just on the variety of teas grown by Kenyan farmers. Below the essay's masthead stood a photo of a Masai woman serving herself tea: cups and jugs and tea bags on a square stainless-steel tray. He said hi to his dad, and walked up to his mom, who was sitting at the dining table reading the Bible. She asked what he would like for his birthday.

'Books.'

'Books?'

'Binyavangaaaa.'

It's Ciru calling. Her little voice tried to pull her big brother outside to see the butterflies she was knitting. Her fingers hurt from the needles and yarns. Both of her thumbs were dark with blood.

Binyavanga did not answer her call.

'Binyavangaaaa.' She called out again.

'Coma?'

'Yes.'

How long do people stay in a coma? Do they hear when we talk to them? Is a coma the end of chaos, or a thoroughfare that leads to an accelerated beginning?

Binyavangaaaa. Open your eyes a little. See the butterflies in your bed. They are the colors of your hair. Some of them are sitting on the intravenous drip. They bear the colours of your imagination. They fly the richness of your love and vulnerability. Some are standing on your hospital gown, flapping little wings; these ones seem alive in the wavelength of the medicines and fluids. The butterflies are leaving powder on your shiny face, your greying beard. What are they doing to you?

Please answer one of us. Say something. Or have you arrived at the end of language?

Ciru was calling me from Nairobi. I was asleep, my phone was off. I waited for the call until chaos shook me and diminished my language. I fell asleep.

Four minutes later, I was awake.

Ciru.

'Hi Ciru.'

'Hi.'

'I missed your calls. Is everything okay?'

'We lost him.'

'Ciru. Ciru. You say?'

'Binya just passed away.' ∎

JAPANESE WIVES

Noriko Hayashi

'It was a sunny day in April 1960. I took a ship to *Chōsen* [Korea] from the port of Niigata, a north-western city of Japan. When I saw my mother for the last time, she was crying. She kept saying, "Please don't go . . . Please change your mind." Every time I remember that moment, I can't help but cry. I was only twenty-one years old.'

In her room in the port city of Wonsan in North Korea, Mitsuko Minakawa sighs while holding a folded handkerchief. She was born in 1939 in Tokyo and was raised in Sapporo. After graduating from high school, Mitsuko enrolled at Hokkaido University – she was the only female student among the one hundred students in her class. In the second year, Mitsuko met a Korean man, Choe Hwa Jae, and fell in love.

In the 1950s, there were about 600,000 Koreans living in Japan. At that time, some of them succeeded in business and gained an education, but the majority were disadvantaged legally and socially, suffering from poverty, as well as ethnic and occupational discrimination. As of December 1954, the total unemployment rate for Koreans in Japan was about eight times the total unemployment rate for the Japanese.

One year later, married, Mitsuko and Hwa Jae decided to leave for North Korea, participating in the massive 'repatriation program' from Japan to North Korea that took place between 1959 and 1984. According to the Japanese Red Cross Society, 93,340 people moved to North Korea during that period, the vast majority of whom were Zainichi Koreans (ethnic Koreans who are permanent residents of Japan). However, that number also includes about 1,800 'Japanese wives' (Japanese women who married Zainichi Koreans) and a small number of 'Japanese husbands' who accompanied the 'returnees'.

In August 1948, the Republic of Korea had been founded in the southern part of the Korean peninsula, and the Democratic People's Republic of Korea in the north the following month. Though more than 95 per cent of the Koreans who moved to North Korea were originally from the southern part of the Korean peninsula, they returned to the north, welcomed by the Democratic People's Republic, which hoped to rebuild the country after the Korean War and to demonstrate the superiority of the socialist system over South Korea.

Mitsuko has now lived in North Korea for almost sixty years. She can see the sea from the window of her room, and Japan across from that sea. Many returnees thought that the unification of the Koreas might happen in the near future, so that they would be able to go back and forth between the north and south. The Japanese wives who crossed the sea also believed that they would be able to move freely between Japan and North Korea after a few years. This would prove untrue.

Since 2013, I have travelled to North Korea twelve times and interviewed and photographed eight Japanese wives in Pyongyang, Wonsan and Hamhung. Three of them have passed away during this period. I realized that they shared a common desire: to visit their hometowns in Japan. I decided to take pictures of the special places they held in their memories and print large photographs onto tarpaulin fabric.

I showed these prints to the Japanese wives and took photos of them observing images of their hometowns: the parks, beaches and shrines. Their reactions were varied. Ms Suzuki quietly approached the print and kept looking at it for a long time. Ms Ota suddenly smiled and kept touching the print. Ms Arai sat in the formal Japanese *seiza* style in front of the print.

Human memory is fragmentary, delicate and complex. This year will be the sixtieth spring that Mitsuko spends in Wonsan. She looks at the sea and says, 'Every May, the acacia flowers are in full bloom here and I can see them from my home. Their scent enters the window when I open it. Each time I smell them, I remember my hometown of Sapporo.' ■

花見によく行った
円山公園の サクラ

花よりだんご

ALL IMAGES © NORIKO HAYASHI / PANOS PICTURES

The magazine of Chatham House covering international affairs

A resource for governments, businesses and academics since 1945

Fresh thinking on the way the world is run and how to improve it

The World Today

Subscribe today and stay informed

theworldtoday.org   +44 (0)20 3544 9725

THE SECOND CAREER OF MICHAEL RIEGELS

Oliver Bullough

As our Embraer EMB-120 twin-turboprop commuter plane gradually levelled off in the balmy Caribbean evening, the vibrations from the propellers rattled different cabin objects in turn: the window blinds; the cockpit door; the cups. The plane-proud steward appeared to be auditioning for a role on a far larger aircraft. 'The captain has extinguished the seat-belt sign. You may now move around the cabin,' he said. There were only twenty-six of us, and no one took him up on the offer. But then, it was so noisy I was probably the only person who could hear.

We were flying north-west, and islands came and went below us, each rimmed with a white surf border. These are the Leeward Islands. Seen from above, they are a singular geographical phenomenon, illustrated so clearly it could be a picture in a school textbook: what happens when two tectonic plates grind against each other and volcanoes burst out along the seam.

Humans are more complex than volcanoes, however, and have divided the singular geographical phenomenon into perhaps the most plural jurisdictional web in the world: independent Antigua; France's St Barts; St Martin, which the French share with the Dutch, who call it Sint Maarten, and which welcomed our overflying Embraer with a text message saying I could use my phone with no extra charge;

Britain's Anguilla, where another text message, a minute or two later, said calls would cost £1.20 a minute; the US Virgin Islands, sold to Washington by the Danes a century ago; and finally, as our plane dipped back under the clouds, and its juddering engines played a new scale on a fresh range of resonant objects, a fresh spray of islets. Seven different jurisdictions, five different countries, all overflown in a forty-five-minute hop.

'Please stow your tray tables for landing,' the steward said, although the plane was not large enough to have any. We skimmed so low over the water we could see through the windows of a luxury housing development on a clifftop. We had arrived in one of Britain's most contested, confusing and consequential outposts: the British Virgin Islands.

The British flag once flew over imperial possessions the length and width of the triangular Caribbean Sea, from Guyana in the south to the Bahamas in the north, then west to tiny Belize on Mexico's southern border. The first Brits in the Caribbean were privateers for Queen Elizabeth, legalised pirates preying on treasure ships sailing from South America to Spain. British colonists then turned to slavery: buying, selling and owning people, establishing control over anywhere that would grow sugar. Even after the slaves were freed in 1834, emancipation was at best partial: thousands upon thousands of black people spent another century in the heat of the tropics, cutting cane for the profit of a handful of white masters.

The sun finally began to set on the empire of sugar in the 1950s. Most of the colonies broke free from Britain, but a handful of them were too small, remote and underpopulated to be turned into independent countries: Montserrat, Anguilla, the Cayman Islands, the Turks and Caicos Islands and – my destination on that rackety plane – the BVI.

None of these places were exactly prosperous, but the BVI were long particularly destitute, and what trade they had was almost entirely with the US-owned islands next door. That economic dependence resulted in the British islands looking markedly more American than any of the other colonies in the Caribbean. 'In fact, the only elements obviously British . . . are the Union Jack that flies over the government buildings and the charming British colonel who is the commissioner,' wrote an American academic who visited in the mid-1950s.

The situation is little changed now. The street signs are of the American type, with boxy white letters on green rectangles. The cars are large and mostly American-made, with automatic transmissions and steering wheels on the left. The currency is the US dollar. In the ex-British islands further south in the Caribbean, such as St Lucia and Dominica, the banknotes retain the Queen's head, but here – on supposedly British territory – you find only greenbacks, with their portraits of US presidents. During a week's stay in the islands, I asked many local people I met if they felt themselves to be British, and most were baffled by the question. They are BVIslanders, they said, as reflected in their official status as 'British Overseas Territories Citizens' – they have a British passport, but have no automatic right to live and work in the UK.

The only unambiguous sign of Britishness I found – if you exclude the flag outside the governor's house – was the crown on a traditional cast-iron pillar box abandoned in the undergrowth. It was a long time since anyone had used it to send a message, however, unless you count those left by dogs.

This local indifference towards London has long been reciprocated. British officials appreciated Antigua for the sheltered port which allowed the Royal Navy to dominate the seas; British businessmen loved Jamaica, Barbados and Trinidad for the profit their sugar brought; but London only kept the Virgin Islands to stop someone else from having them. They had no military significance and, as soon as the slaves were freed in the 1830s, there was no profit for planters here either. When the islands stopped being profitable, Britain lost interest in its colony.

The colonists went elsewhere, and their no-longer-required

labourers were left to themselves, which marked the end of the first phase of empire for these islands, and the beginning of the second. The left-behind people lived off littoral fishing, cattle farming and subsistence agriculture, and they did so for a century or more, deep into the second half of the twentieth century.

But the islands never stopped being nominally British, and that was attraction enough for Michael Riegels, who is a straight-backed, white-haired, aquiline-nosed man of a type that is now all but extinct: someone who is unmistakably English, but who barely knows England. He was born eighty-one years ago in what was then Tanganyika, one of the many colonies where a Brit could make a good living without having to tolerate the rain, pollution and squalor of life in the 'mother country'. But such places became rare: Britain's footprint grew smaller and, in 1961, his birth country became the independent Tanzania.

Michael's wife Norma served us curry East Africa-style – with fresh chutneys of banana and onion – before they settled down to describe how they ended up in the Caribbean. They had stuck it out in Dar es Salaam for more than a decade after independence, but life became increasingly difficult as the post-colonial government built a China-aligned, one-party state. 'If you did something the government didn't like, they put you in permanent detention, you just disappeared,' Norma explained. 'It got to the stage, our son was almost a year old, when Michael would say: "If I'm not home by seven o'clock, get out on the next plane." One day came and we said: "We can't live like this any more." So we went back to the UK. We hated it, had another baby.'

That was in 1973, perhaps the most dispiriting year in a dispiriting decade for Britain: a year of strikes, IRA bombings, the oil crisis and the three-day week. It was a miserable time for pretty much everyone, but particularly so for a young couple accustomed to the warmth and exuberance of East Africa who were trying to start life again, having been forced by exchange controls to leave a lifetime's savings behind them and who had two young children to feed.

Michael was a barrister and heard from a friend about a law firm looking for a new partner in the British Virgin Islands. He'd never heard of the place, but anywhere had to be better than where they were. He came out to have a look, saw the sun on the water, felt the warmth on his skin and fell in love immediately. So he and Norma packed their belongings, gathered up the kids and shipped out for a new life on a third continent in as many years. 'When we came here from Tanzania, we thought we'd died and gone to heaven,' Michael remembered. 'It was so nice. And it was a change not having everyone saying you're a filthy imperialist swine, which does get wearing after a while.'

Britain had lost an empire and Michael Riegels had found a role, one that would make him a fortune and propel this lost little colony to the centre of the modern world. Riegels and the BVI were going into the incorporation business.

The United States and Britain had a treaty under which they agreed not to tax each other's companies' profits. Such double-taxation treaties are foundational to the globalised economy because they ensure that a company that operates in more than one country isn't taxed twice on the same money. Riegels's new business was based on the fact that this treaty extended to Britain's overseas colonies, which exposed a flaw at the heart of this system: if one country undercuts the other on tax rates, companies that base themselves there can dramatically reduce the amount of tax they pay in the other.

Most big countries won't play this game, because it would destroy their tax bases. The BVI, being small and having a weak economy, had no such considerations because it didn't have much tax revenue to lose: the new business the islands attracted from relocating companies gained them more in fees than they lost in taxes. Such countries are now understood and referred to as tax havens, but back in the 1970s they were a new phenomenon and businesses were exploring them with relish.

In the 1970s, corporations in the BVI paid 15 per cent tax on their profits, while in the United States they paid 50 per cent. If an

American incorporated her business in the Caribbean she could export her dividends and cut her effective tax rate by more than half. All she needed was a local lawyer. And, dating from 1976, when US clients first found him, that lawyer was Michael Riegels.

This was not just lucrative for the businesswoman in question, who was cutting her tax rate by 35 percentage points, and not just good business for Riegels, whose law firm expanded fast. It was also fantastic for the government of the British Virgin Islands. At the time, most islanders were still subsistence farmers. The islands' government was so poor that it was powerless to develop the economy and was constantly obliged to beg London for funds, and so welcomed any fresh revenue.

Each company that Riegels created brought a fee into the BVI's administrative budget. The more companies that were created, the more fees there were; the more fees that were paid, the more funds the government had to spend. It didn't care if it was thereby enabling tax dodging in other countries, depriving their governments of revenue; it cared about finally having an income and being able to build some roads and hire some teachers. The BVI business model didn't bear much moral scrutiny, but needs must: it was all that was available and it proved a successful way of putting food on the table. By 1978, the islands no longer needed 'grant-in-aid', the subsidies to their budget sent from London. They had become financially self-sufficient.

'It started off quite slowly, then it picked up,' Riegels said with wry understatement. 'By the time the US pulled the plug on us, it was quite a few: a hundred companies a month.'

Not every lawyer manages to enrage the US government, but Riegels succeeded with the diligent and reliable way he created companies for Americans. In 1982, the United States, infuriated by the BVI's flagrant enabling of massive tax avoidance, cancelled the islands' access to the double-taxation treaty and thus removed the key advantage of their business model. The islands' administration, which had become rather attached to picking the Americans' pockets, was stunned. Riegels remembers local premier Hamilton Lavity Stoutt asking him to find a way around what the Americans had done. The BVI might still be a colony, which meant that the UK government could overrule the local administration on any matter it wanted, but the islands also had their own assembly, which meant they could pass their own laws. It was an uneasy compromise between colonialism and democracy, and here it worked to the lawyers' advantage.

The US lawyers who had been sending Riegels most of his work had an idea: they said, 'What you guys really need is a very good companies act, very user-friendly, flexible, commercially attractive, so you can wind companies up quickly, can form companies quickly, so you can have one shareholder.' Deregulate, deregulate, deregulate. It was very much in keeping with the political tone of the times. Britain and America were deregulating, business was being unleashed, greed was good, the empire of money was replacing the empires of politics, a tsunami of footloose capital was crashing onto the world and the BVI was going to surf that wave.

Lawyers drew up the bill and presented it to the BVI parliament. 'It passed in a day, unanimous. No one had a clue what it meant probably,' Riegels remembered. The new law was technical and complicated, but created something genuinely new: the international business company, a hyper-deregulated shell corporation. The companies were not taxed at all, which made them highly attractive to business people, and there was no registry of who actually owned them, which was a matter for individual lawyers. With one of these IBCs, you could own property anywhere, pay no tax and operate with complete anonymity.

It was an idea whose time had come, thanks to two coincidental favours from history. The first boon was Britain's announcement in 1984 that it would hand control of Hong Kong back to China in 1997. A lot of wealthy people were very concerned that their property would be expropriated and sought a way to move ownership of that property overseas, thus hiding it from Beijing. 'All the Chinamen got a terrible fright and said: "We've got to move our assets out." And somehow the BVI sprang into someone's head. Now in Hong Kong they talk about having a BVI, everyone has a BVI,' Riegels told me.

The second boon was Washington's decision to invade Panama and expel Manuel Noriega. Panama had been the base for some of the muckiest business in the Americas, and the lawyers who had been arranging that business suddenly found themselves needing a new home. They found that home – for both themselves and their clients' business – in Road Town. This meant the British Virgin Islands had become the haven of choice for both Asian businessmen looking to hide their activities from Beijing and criminals looking to hide their activities from the FBI. The BVI might have lost the US tax-dodging business, but it more than replaced it with these new revenue streams, particularly since they both turned out to be two of the biggest growth areas of the decades ahead. From 1989, when Noriega was ousted, new incorporations increased every year by 50 per cent. By 1999, the BVI had more than two-fifths of the world's entire market for offshore companies. These islands had gone from being barely a backwater to a key hub in the globalised economy in a single generation.

Every company created, whoever bought it, generated fees for the government. So it was in the government's interests not to ask too many questions about where the money came from, or what the companies were being used for. Those fees make up two-thirds of the BVI budget, paying for roads, schools, the hospital and police officers' wages. BVIslanders stopped farming cassava and goats, and started importing frozen chicken and potatoes. Everyone got a share, and it was all thanks to Riegels.

'We do a good job, we've always tried to be efficient, which is a bit of a struggle in the Caribbean. The idea of doing something instantly is not very Caribbean. But to give the BVI its due, it offered a very good service at a very reasonable price. I don't say we're cheap, we're just good value for money,' he said.

Riegels is long retired now and lives in a villa situated high above the sea and facing a little east of south. After he had finished telling me about how he invented the world's most prolific offshore tax haven, we sat on his terrace and looked down onto the Sir Francis

Drake Channel, and beyond that to the chain of smaller islands that separate Tortola from the Atlantic Ocean. The sun danced on the water, lighting up the sails of the white yachts running into Road Town with the trade wind. It was deliciously warm and delightfully diverting. There was always something to see, every minute was different, while the breeze ruffled the surface of our cups of tea and blew the hair off my forehead. Just the day before Norma had seen a three-masted yacht which, according to her neighbour, who read about it on Facebook, had cost its Russian owner more than $300 million.

It felt a long way from Dar es Salaam, with its grim East German-style government assistance programme, and just as far from suburban London, with its gossip and curtains and culs-de-sac. 'It was fortuitous. I could still be sitting in Ham or somewhere in England, bitching about the weather and Brexit and everything else,' Michael said, laughing hugely. 'But here I couldn't care less.'

Although Riegels's invention was significant in the way it supported the islands' budget and gave them fiscal independence from Britain, the actual process of what he did every day was not in and of itself very interesting. Company incorporations are the krill at the bottom of the financial food chain: they are enormously numerous and cumulatively valuable, but also quite dull. Requests come in, forms are completed, fees are paid, companies go out – low margin, high volume. The clients might be interesting, the money may or may not be crooked, but the job is not. However, as with krill, when companies emerge in vast quantities, the effects are extraordinary.

The BVI works hard to explain that those effects are beneficial, that its companies are a win-win-win for everyone in the world, that they build prosperity at home, spread capital around, and create jobs everywhere. According to a recent report, written for the islands by a business consultancy firm, $1.5 trillion of investment has been 'mediated' by BVI companies, creating some 2.2 million jobs, most of them in the Far East, 12,000 of them in the United

States. 'Uninformed individuals and organisations have questioned our integrity and approach,' the report said. 'However, we stand firm in the belief that international finance centres like ours service very specific business needs, bringing together a network of skilled professionals with deep technical knowledge and a specialist financial services infrastructure.'

BVI companies provide anonymity, convenience, respectability – all for a very reasonable price. They are quantum objects, which project the laws of one country into the space of another, to the benefit of those wealthy enough to afford their services. You can own your assets wherever you want to, wrap them in an offshore company, and the laws of your home country cannot follow you inside. If you are struggling to understand how this works, that's because it doesn't make sense. The illogicality of shell companies is a result of the fact that they emerged from an illogical system in which globalisation is incomplete: money can go anywhere, but laws cannot. And the consequences of that mismatch are profound. They have helped major corporations reduce their tax burdens, depriving treasuries everywhere of revenue. They have smoothed the path of capitalism, stripping away the tiresome regulations insisted on by governments elsewhere. And, on the way, they have helped hide the identities of the people behind a new form of colonialism. It was once Europeans who looted Africa, Asia and the Americas of their wealth and brought it home to spend on luxuries. Now those continents' own rulers do the looting as well, and the money ends up in the same cities as it always did. We struggle to find out about it, because it's hidden behind the convenient anonymity provided by shell companies.

Here's an example: in 1999, the ceasefire in Angola's civil war was precarious. On one side, UNITA was funded by the trade in illegally mined diamonds; on the other side, the MPLA earned its living from oil. Angola was once a front in the Cold War – the West's UNITA against the USSR's MPLA – but by the 1990s, ideological differences were long forgotten and the war was all about controlling resources, and making as much profit as possible for the individuals leading the two sides. Ordinary Angolans, meanwhile, were some of the poorest people anywhere: rates of disease, maternal mortality, premature death and malnutrition were extremely high.

The 1999 ceasefire gave some hope that the war would end and ordinary Angolans would begin to gain some respite. Leading figures from the MPLA, however, had other plans. They created a company in the BVI called CADA, which 'won' a five-year $720 million contract to supply its armed forces with food and uniforms. Then the ceasefire broke down and the two sides went back to war, to the personal profit of the MPLA leaders who owned CADA and who stood to make personal fortunes selling food and uniforms to their own party's soldiers. Angolans were dying, their country was being devastated and the country's rulers were able to store the tax-free, anonymous profits they made from the destruction they themselves perpetrated behind the protective screen of a BVI company. The leaders of the MPLA poured this money into luxury goods and property in London and Lisbon, free from scrutiny or interference.

It could have been a scandal for the ages, but it barely scratched the public consciousness, anywhere. It was just one example of egregious corruption among many others; just one shell company among millions.

We know about this case thanks to a report written by Global Witness, a campaigning organisation founded in London in 1993 to publicise the links between corruption, human rights abuses and natural resources, particularly in developing countries. All over the world, and at an accelerating rate, the rulers of the poorest countries were acting just like the MPLA in Angola, using their political power to amass vast wealth, which they then hid behind shell companies, spending capital with impunity in London, New York, Paris and other Western centres. Global Witness activists hoped that by exposing what was happening, they could force governments to clean up. They were not entirely unsuccessful, particularly with their focus in 1998 on 'blood diamonds', a term they invented, which helped bring in a certification system for precious stones. But corruption was spreading all across Asia, Africa, South America, the former Soviet Union and the Middle East, bringing misery with it.

'We used the metaphor of the leaky bucket in campaigning on corruption – that pouring aid into countries is like pouring water into a leaky bucket if flight capital is coming the other way,' said Anthea Lawson, an experienced campaigner who saw the damage the blood diamond trade did in Sierra Leone when working against the arms trade with a local NGO. 'I had a strong sense that the world was run for, by and on behalf of a very small proportion of its population.'

In 2006, she joined Global Witness to focus on this problem, which was a new departure for the NGO. For the first time it had hired someone specifically to look at the way that the revenue from corrupt assets was hidden and where it was spent. Once Lawson had understood what was happening, Global Witness wanted to use her findings to force governments to shut those networks down. It had become too easy for crooked people to obscure their activities, to hide and spend their cash, and too many lawyers were willing to help them do so.

'They told me to turn it all around into a report on what banks are doing, to get it out in three months,' is how she remembers the exchange. The work ended up being far more complicated than anyone had anticipated. 'It took two years, five months and seven days. Not three months.'

When she dug through a hard drive salvaged from Liberia, she found secret financial records from Congo-Brazzaville: there were bank accounts in Hong Kong, shell companies in the Caribbean and much more. Global Witness called the report 'Undue Diligence: How banks do business with corrupt regimes' and it was revolutionary.

It singled out some of the world's biggest financial institutions – Barclays, Citibank, Deutsche Bank – for criticism; it slated the failure of Western countries to prevent their financial systems being used to legitimise stolen money and proposed new rules to drive dirty money out of the world economy. The explosive charge, however, was buried on page six, in the first bullet point below point four: 'Each country should publish an online registry of the beneficial ownership of all companies and trusts.' Again, that doesn't sound like much, but it demanded that anyone, anywhere, should be able to discover the true owner of a company. Only then could we be sure that crooks were not hiding their theft behind shell corporations and only then could we be confident that theft would be exposed. There wasn't a single country in the world that met that test – Lawson was demanding a radical overhaul in the way globalisation works. She was also posing a clear and present danger to the BVI's business model: if the ownership of the islands' companies was visible to anyone, why would people incorporate there?

A friend at Global Witness had asked me, while I was visiting the islands, to check out five BVI companies which featured on a couple of contracts for mining operations in Afghanistan and to see if I could find out anything about them. On the third day after my arrival, I set out to make some enquiries.

There is a standard playbook for journalists looking to investigate companies in the BVI. You start with an official document containing the name of one or more BVI companies, such as the contract provided by my Global Witness friend. Each company should have an address, which will be that of its 'registered agent', the law firm that created it, looks after it and answers post on its behalf. That registered agent will have a file that contains the name of the company's real owner. The journalist's ambition is to get hold of that file.

The main island in the BVI is Tortola. It is twelve miles long with a rocky spine, like a swimming dragon. I was staying on the north coast, in a cabin overlooking a tiny sandy cove, and had to drive over the island's ridge, then down the precipitous road towards the other shore. From the top you looked onto the port of Road Town, home to 13,000 of the islands' 31,000 or so people.

The first company on my list was registered at Drake Chambers in the Yamraj building, a sunflower-yellow block surrounded by street traders selling food from stalls in a ramshackle car park. No one in the building had ever heard of Drake Chambers, or if they had they weren't prepared to tell me about it, so that search got me nowhere. Strike one.

The second company was registered at Craigmuir Chambers, a ten-minute walk away, and based in the same building as Harneys, the large law firm where Michael Riegels had once been a partner. This was a more professional operation, with an air-conditioned lobby and a rank of receptionists in headsets answering calls as they came in. Here at least they admitted that the chambers existed, though they wouldn't let me past the front desk to look for myself. A friendly receptionist with a cap of tight grey curls made a call on my behalf, then she handed me the phone and watched calmly as an American-accented staffer explained that he could not possibly allow me access to the company files without permission from the company's owners.

'That would not be possible, sir. Permission from the company has to be received in writing,' he explained.

I would, of course, not be able to obtain that permission, since I didn't know who the owners were and therefore couldn't ask them. Catch-22. Strike two.

You begin to see the point of this exercise. Every journalist who comes here knows in advance that they won't really be able to extract any information from this round of visits, that the files containing the company owner's names will remain closed to them, but these repeated conversations demonstrate the opacity of the place: the number of people employed to keep secrets for – in this case – possibly corrupt Afghan government officials, and thus the inherently criminogenic nature of the BVI's business model. The point is to inflict humiliation on the enablers of corruption by forcing them to admit in person that they won't help journalists who are seeking to expose crimes.

The law firms know the playbook too, of course. Not many journalists come here, but pretty much every one who does has trekked along these same pavements and knocked on the same doors. It is the receptionists who bear the brunt of this process, which is unfortunate, since that means journalistic humiliation is inflicted on low-paid local women, rather than on the high-earning foreign men who actually make the profits from creating the companies. It feels a bit like waging war by shooting conscripts rather than their officers, but it is the playbook nonetheless and it must be followed because there isn't an alternative.

Or rather there didn't used to be an alternative. In 2015, someone – their identity remains unknown – leaked 2.6 terabytes of data, which is 11.5 million computer files, from the database of a Panamanian law firm called Mossack Fonseca to two German journalists. Those journalists shared their trove with colleagues all over the world, resulting in the media sensation known as the Panama Papers. Exhaustively analysed over many months, then published in a coordinated global journalistic blitzkrieg, the legal documents exposed misbehaviour by high-ranking officials from Russia, Ukraine, Pakistan, Iraq, Egypt and elsewhere. They established firmly in the public mind the connection between the offshore financial system and grand kleptocratic corruption and tax dodging. They also exposed the ownership of the more than 100,000 BVI companies for which Mossack Fonseca was the registered agent.

Before the Panama Papers, the Road Town office of Mossack Fonseca would have been a scheduled stop on the playbook tour. A journalist might theoretically have called in and asked the receptionist about the ownership of Sandalwood Continental Ltd, a company that received $57.6 million from a huge Russian money-laundering scheme; or Pan World Investments Inc., which appeared to have suspicious ties in the Middle East. Before 2016, the receptionist would have handed out the standard brush-off, told the journalist that the information was confidential and could only be disclosed with the company's written permission. But now we know that those companies belonged, respectively, to a close friend of Vladimir Putin – a cellist named Sergei Roldugin – and Alaa Mubarak, the son of Egypt's former president. The Panama Papers was like suddenly being able to walk past the receptionist and open any file you wanted.

They were also a tremendous blow to Mossack Fonseca's reputation. Not only did the firm become a synonym for the worst kind of offshore skulduggery, but the scandal also shredded its appeal for potential clients: why would anyone entrust their secrets to a company that had so spectacularly failed to keep them? The law firm finally closed in March 2018 and boarded up the three-storey sky-blue building that had been its BVI centre of operations. The company name has been removed from its facade – although, for reasons that are obscure, the terminal 'k' of Mossack and the initial 'F' of Fonseca have been left behind, and you can still read the whole name in ghostly grey plaster. This is appropriate: Mossack Fonseca may have gone, but the spirit of the Caribbean's most notorious law firm haunts the BVI still.

The walk to the third stop on my journalistic tour took me past Mossack Fonseca's former front door. I was looking for the Little Denmark building. It has a shop on the ground floor selling gifts to tourists – pirate T-shirts, cheap sunglasses, little bits of plastic embossed with slogans about rum – and a law firm upstairs that was the registered agent for one of the companies on my list. I climbed up the external staircase and knocked on the door. At first, things played out according to the script: the receptionist told me, in her honeyed Caribbean accent, that she couldn't help me without permission from the company in question. But then something unexpected happened: a white middle-aged British lawyer emerged from his office and walked over for a chat.

'Why don't you try the company registry?' he said, and gave me detailed instructions on how to find it. A company registry? A helpful lawyer? This was new. This was not in the playbook at all.

In 2016, British prime minister David Cameron hosted a global anti-corruption summit. The summit itself was rather overshadowed: firstly by the Panama Papers scandal, and the revelation that Cameron himself had profited from an offshore trust; and secondly by the Brexit referendum, and the subsequent end to Cameron's career. But the summit was important, thanks to a promise the BVI made to collate information on who actually owned its companies and to make that information available to the British police.

The new system required two new databases: the Virtual Integrated Registry and Regulatory General Information Network (VIRRGIN), which allowed companies to file their documents; and the Beneficial Ownership Secure Search (BOSS) system, which allowed that information to be searched. It is the latter that the helpful lawyer pointed me towards, the repository of information about who actually owns the companies registered here. It included the five names listed on the piece of paper given to me by my Global Witness friend, and which was by now rather damp since I'd been holding it in my hand all morning. The system itself is housed in a steel-framed shed a mile or so from the town centre, and its gatekeeper – the boss of the BOSS, as it were – was a warm grandmotherly computer operator. She sat behind a chest-high desk in a room to the right of the entrance hall and was, when I arrived, gossiping with a colleague. It was her job to check the registry on my behalf. I wrote down the company names on an official request form and she typed them into her directory. The whole process took about fifteen minutes.

I did not exactly come away with much. For each of the five companies, I got a list of the documents BOSS has on file, almost all of which I could not access. This small trove of information cost me $165, so it wasn't cheap, and it left me no wiser about the true owners of the firms involved in the mining contract in Afghanistan. Nonetheless, it was a step forward, and positively transparent compared to what I have been able to access in other tax havens (in Nevis, for example, a little island to the south of the BVI, it's impossible to receive confirmation that a company even exists, let alone see what information exists about it). British police officers, as well as anyone who can prove a 'legitimate interest' – normally in relation to court proceedings – have full access to all the information. They can see who actually owns companies here, which means the British Virgin Islands is no longer the haven of secrecy that it used to be.

This is probably why the number of new companies incorporated on the islands has dropped sharply, from more than 77,000 in 2007 to fewer than 33,000 in 2017. Maybe the dodgy operators have moved their business to places more inclined to keep their secrets: Nevis, Delaware, Nevada. One lawyer in Road Town certainly thought so.

'The really sophisticated crooks, the Russians, for example, they're long gone,' he said. 'We still have some stupid people, corrupt Brazilians, for example, and they're always really surprised when they get caught. "I thought the BVI was supposed to be a tax haven" – that sort of thing.'

Whisper it, but, thanks to the BOSS system, the BVI's government was starting to earn a respectable living.

After the publication of her 2009 investigation, Anthea Lawson took her ideas on the road. She addressed members of the US House of Representatives, she spoke to the British Parliament and her idea about transparency as a solution to kleptocracy began to catch on. That same year, the Tax Justice Network published its first Financial Secrecy Index, which analyses jurisdictions by how transparent they are; and journalists started to look more closely at how corporations moved profits to low-tax jurisdictions. By 2010, a coalition of dozens of NGOs demanded that the G20 commit to making ownership information a matter of public record.

This was in the immediate aftermath of the financial crisis, when successive revelations of tax avoidance by multinational companies – often via the same kinds of offshore structures favoured by the kleptocrats – coincided with government austerity policies. Public anger about this perceived unfairness welled up in movements like Occupy and UK Uncut.

In 2014, Global Witness won a prize from TED, the organisation which stages the hugely prestigious annual conference and where attendees pay thousands of dollars to sit in a room and hear about ideas that will improve the world. Anthea Lawson's boss – Global Witness co-founder Charmian Gooch – spoke at the main conference in Vancouver, and Anthea herself was invited to speak at a spin-off conference in London. Both of them made ownership transparency the centrepiece of their presentations, and endorsement from TED showed quite clearly that this was an idea whose time had come.

The impact of the idea of ownership transparency has been extraordinary: from Lawson's initial report in 2009, to testimony before Parliament, to street protests, to the world's most famous ideas conference and finally to British government policy, all in the space of seven years. A wonky accountancy concept had become one of the hottest governance issues in the world and the BVI had stopped being an impregnable fortress of secrecy, thanks to the BOSS system.

There was still a problem, however, which was that although BOSS provided far more information on company ownership than that available in other tax havens, activists and journalists still did not have free access to it. Cameron had wanted to impose full transparency, but had been forced to compromise and accept the islands' desire to restrict information only to those with a legal right to see it. In a practical sense, the compromise was sensible. Simply opening up the BVI registry was pointless because the dodgy shell companies would just relocate somewhere else.

Normally, this kind of wonky policy discussion would have continued within the offices of Whitehall, and caution would have prevailed. Relations with the remaining colonies are a matter for the Foreign Office, perhaps the most conservative of all of Britain's government departments. Steady, slow, incremental progress would be made; diplomatic precedent would be respected. But post-referendum Britain does not follow normal rules. The government had no majority in Parliament and the ties that link parties together are fraying. A group of MPs refused to settle for second best.

'We cannot sit here and ignore the practices that allow Britain and our British overseas territories to provide safe havens for dirty money. If we can act to root out the corruption, we must do so,' insisted Margaret Hodge, a Labour MP and a veteran campaigner against the abuses of the financial system, on 1 May 2018. In partnership with Andrew Mitchell, a Conservative who in normal times would have been her political enemy, she was proposing an amendment that would force the BVI to open up. They had become the leaders of a loose group of MPs, and they were winning.

Government ministers tried to argue that Britain needed to respect the autonomy of its overseas territories. They pointed out that if the BVI opened up entirely, the dirty business would just go away. But this is British politics now, there is no tolerance for compromise. 'It is a little bit like the battle against malaria,' said Mitchell. 'We should bring the same vigour and determination to the fight against poisoned money as we do to the fight against deadly insects.'

That is an alarming metaphor, suggesting that the proposal's effects would be the same as dousing Britain's remaining colonies in insecticide, but the government folded and accepted them anyway. Suddenly, without plan or preparation, Britain was launching the BVI onto a fourth phase in its relationship with London. Phase one had been slavery, phase two was neglect, phase three brought shell companies, and now came a slap: no one in London appeared to know what the effects would be, or to much care.

London's representative in the British Virgin Islands is the governor, who works out of a quietly attractive two-storey white villa on the edge of Road Town. The current governor is Augustus James Ulysses Jaspert, a career diplomat who was sworn in in August 2017, and who is apparently better known as Gus, though I didn't personally get onto those kinds of terms with him. I had a meeting arranged with him for mid-morning and parked my car in a tiny patch of shade that I hoped would still be there when I got back. I rang the bell to get past the green-painted fence, walked across a pleasant little garden and rang again to enter the lobby, where I was instructed to wait.

I sat for a while, scrutinising a plaque bearing the names of all the governors of the BVI since 1956. A steady stutter of people went outside for a smoke, asking me if I was being taken care of each time, so I changed to a seat further from the door and examined a portrait of the Queen, in which she strongly resembled my mother-in-law. I leafed through the literature in a wall-mounted magazine rack: a dog-eared flyer for an American insurance company, a three-year-old copy of a BVI finance pamphlet and a 2017 glossy about Britain's best brands. It felt like the staff common room at a failing prep school in Herefordshire; it did not feel like the nerve centre of the Caribbean outpost of a modern and forward-facing country.

Eventually, I was invited upstairs and ushered into the governor's presence. Jaspert was pink-faced and sandy-haired, not quite forty years old, with an appropriate handshake. I would love to tell you what he said, but he made me promise that our meeting was off the record before we sat down. Don't feel too left out, however. Our meeting began ten minutes late, consisted entirely of platitudes and ended when one of his underlings appeared to tell him he had 'a call'. If he told me anything that was worth putting on the record during the five minutes or so we spent at the same table I failed to notice it. I was back outside so quickly that the last two office smokers hadn't even finished their cigarettes by the time I walked past them.

Jaspert has had a tough time since taking on the job. In 2017, Hurricane Irma devastated the islands within weeks of his arrival, causing tens of millions of pounds of damage. There were wrecked yachts in semi-submerged drifts in many of Tortola's bays, and the islanders were still struggling to obtain the money and building materials they needed to repair their roofs and windows. The UK Parliament's vote imposing transparency on the islands followed so shortly after the hurricane that the local premier took to referring to them as twin natural disasters inflicted by outside powers they could not control. Perhaps it was out of concern for the fact he represented London – one of those outside powers – that persuaded the governor not to risk telling me anything. I was left with the lingering feeling that I had offended him somehow.

Jaspert oversees a government formed after elections in February

2019, which resulted in the ejection of the National Democratic Party and their replacement by the Virgin Islands Party. Both parties were opposed to the UK overruling local politicians, and both expressed concern for how the islands would survive the new regime of transparency. In London, however, no one appeared to notice. The islanders' expression of democratic irritation passed entirely unremarked in the House of Commons.

'Mr Speaker, I will liken the above scenario to that of a ship that has sailed and is now contending with tempestuous seas,' the new premier and minister of finance, Andrew Fahie, told the twelve other members of the House of Representatives in his first budget speech in early April 2019. 'The new captain and crew fully accept that for the sustainable future of the ship, at a minimum, there must be a tactical change of direction. Whether the change calls for a trimming of the sails, a diversion from the current course or a decision for a head-on assault is still under active consideration.'

A couple of weeks later I met his deputy, Natalio Wheatley, who holds a doctorate from the University of London's School of Oriental and African Studies, and often goes by the name Sowande Uhuru in recognition of the African heritage of his ancestors, for coffee by the marina in Road Town. He is thirty-nine years old, outspoken, and the heir to a political dynasty – his grandfather was the territory's first minister of finance and second chief minister back in the 1970s. For Wheatley, the biggest frustration was that none of the British politicians who had voted to overrule the local parliament had got in touch to ask him what he thought about it.

'I would love to engage with them. I am familiar with those discussions about corruption and kleptocracy in Africa and so forth, and I don't doubt for one moment that people have used companies for illegitimate purposes. In the same way I don't doubt people have used a knife for illegitimate purposes, or a car. It's just a tool,' he said. Like Anthea Lawson, he has travelled widely in Sierra Leone, seen the damage that corruption has done to the entire fabric of society there and recognises the need to clean up the financial services industry.

But he's accountable to the people who elected him, and they rely on incorporation fees.

'The government's whole operation depends very heavily on the fees from financial services, everything: schools, hospitals, roads, care for the elderly, care for persons with mental challenges. It's almost existential, the threat, based on the open register,' Wheatley said simply.

And yet, in dozens of other countries all of those crucial services are unavailable precisely because the government's revenues are being looted, under the cover of shell companies often registered in the BVI. This is perhaps the whole problem with globalisation and its dark side – kleptocracy. The people harmed by it don't get to vote in the same elections as those who benefit from it: politicians who drive out the dirty money receive no electoral boost for doing so, rather the reverse.

I promised to pass on Wheatley's email address to the activists I know at Global Witness and other groups. I was pretty sure they'd get on, but I wasn't optimistic that anything would come of it. This is a problem that derives from a contradiction at the heart of the world economy: money is transnational, laws are not. And solving this problem requires more than the British Virgin Islands government, or indeed the British government, can deliver. Activists and journalists have highlighted the problem, and have embarrassed those getting rich from it, but they can't resolve it.

The question is: who can? Because surely we can't go on like this. ■

Jack Underwood

The novel

So there's a man, or a woman, okay,
a person, and this person has a problem.
Not so much a problem as a yearning.
They live in a city but yearn for
the quiet of the countryside. No,
they yearn for the geometry, the voltage,
the violent anonymity of the city. Or
they yearn for the selfish, fat simplicity
of their childhood. Okay, something
more specific. They yearn for the silence
that followed the call of the mother-owl
out across the misted glade that morning
in June. Or the silence of a blown-out
filament like a ruined suspension bridge
in a snow globe without snow.
That silence. That is what the person
yearns for. Only they don't know
that this silence is what they yearn for.
Instead they cast around, throwing
their yearning over everything
like holy water, not knowing that
the attainment of surrogate objects
of desire only frustrates or aggravates
their yearning, since the act
of attainment itself eliminates an object
from the category of desire, throwing it
into severe relief, so that immediately
it takes on a figurine aspect,
a repulsive resemblance of the silent

moment that the person does not
know they yearn for. Thus abandoned,
the search continues, the world always
ready with fresh and bright distractions.
And this person is just like us.
It could be us. Only it isn't.
But you do know this person.
I can tell you that much.
Though of course, I needn't tell you.
You know exactly who I'm talking about.

Jack Underwood

This time

it's going to be great! God called out to his wife. – I know I've said it before, but I think I'm really onto something. I'm going to give them a linear sense of time, just one direction, all the way! – What? Mrs God replied, arriving in the doorway where the garage meets the utility room adjoining the kitchen – But that's hardly anything at all? she said, bemused, placing one of two plates with neatly cut sandwiches, each with a pile of assorted accompanying pickles, down on the workbench. – I know! But that way they'll have beginnings and endings! Think how dramatic that will be! They'll need neat little bodies to inhabit, perhaps starting off small and new then growing larger, then more prone to malfunction, until they fail and each of them disappears down the shoot, whoosh! I know it seems like a brutal constraint but it'll create pressure, dynamism, I mean, think how many of them will never meet, lovers kept a thousand years apart by a cruel lottery of ordering! And the great meandering conversations, stratified, strung out across the epochs, new voices, inflections, accents and terminologies joining all the time, just as the older voices and languages slide from memory, one gigantic melting block of ice that none will ever see even a corner of. Just imagine the intensity of that narrowed, sharpened experience. What a trip! God grabbed the sandwich and chewed madly, scrutinising the sketches he had made. – They'll be popping off like champagne bottles, they'll be out of their tiny minds! Mrs God rolled her eyes, taking her identical sandwich and pickles back indoors where the afternoon stretched like a cat between naps.

Not yet a subscriber?

Since 1979, *Granta* has provided a platform for the best new writing. These pages defined the literary genre Dirty Realism, tracked down a deposed South American dictator, documented the fall of Saigon, invented the Best of Young Novelists format, explored the strange world of Chinese cricket fighting, published twenty-seven Nobel laureates and highlighted the literary landscapes of Brazil, Canada, India, Ireland, Japan, Pakistan and Spain.

Don't miss out.

Subscribe now from £34/$42 per year.
Digital subscriptions also available from £12/$16.

Visit granta.com/subscribe for details.

GRANTA

CONTRIBUTORS

Oliver Bullough is a writer and journalist from Wales who specialises in financial crime and the former Soviet Union. He is the author of *Moneyland* and *The Last Man in Russia*.

Michael Collins is a photographer and writer based in London, whose photographs have been exhibited in England, Germany and the US, and are in numerous collections. His most recent book, *The Family Silver*, is drawn from his collection of amateur British family slides.

Pwaangulongii Dauod is the former creative director at Ilmihouse, an art house in Kaduna, Nigeria, and is a 2016 MacDowell Colony fellow. A winner of the Gerald Kraak Prize, he was shortlisted for a Morland Writing Scholarship. He is currently an O'Brien Fellow at McGill University. He is working on a collection of essays, *Africa's Future Has No Space for Stupid Black Men*, and a novel, *A Year of Disgrace*.

Sidik Fofana received an MFA in Creative Writing from NYU and teaches public school in Brooklyn. His work has appeared in the *Sewanee Review*. 'The Young Entrepreneurs of Miss Bristol's Front Porch' is an excerpt from his debut novel, *Stories from Our Tenants Downstairs*, forthcoming

from Scribner in the US and Hodder in the UK in 2021.

Adam Foulds is a poet and novelist. His most recent novel, *Dream Sequence*, was published in 2019.

Noriko Hayashi is a Japanese documentary photographer based in Tokyo. She has been exploring the relationship between Japan and North Korea for close to a decade and 'Japanese Wives' is the latest chapter of this long-term project.

Amy Leach is the author of *Things That Are* and *The Modern Moose*, forthcoming from Farrar, Straus and Giroux in the US. Her work has appeared in *The Best American Essays 2009*, and she has been recognised with a Whiting Award and a Rona Jaffe Foundation Writers' Award.

Mazen Maarouf is a Palestinian-Icelandic writer, poet, translator and journalist, born in Beirut to a family of Palestinian refugees. He has published three collections of poetry and two short-story collections in Arabic. *Jokes for the Gunmen*, published by Granta Books in 2019, was awarded the 2016 Al-Multaqa Prize for the Arabic Short Story and was longlisted for the 2019 Man Booker International Prize.

Carmen Maria Machado is the author of the memoir *In the Dream House* and the story collection *Her Body and Other Parties*. She has been a finalist for the National Book Award and the winner of the Bard Fiction Prize, the Lambda Literary Award for Lesbian Fiction, the Brooklyn Public Library Literature Prize, a Shirley Jackson Award and the National Book Critics Circle's John Leonard Prize. She is the Writer in Residence at the University of Pennsylvania and lives in Philadelphia with her wife.

Andrew O'Hagan is the author of eight books. He is an editor-at-large for the *London Review of Books* and *Esquire*. His forthcoming novel *Mayflies* will be published by Faber & Faber in 2020.

Tommi Parrish is a cartoonist, illustrator and art editor based in Montreal, whose second work and first long-form graphic novel, *The Lie and How We Told It*, was published in 2017.

Jack Underwood's *Happiness* was published by Faber & Faber in 2015. A double-pamphlet *Solo For Mascha Voice/Tenuous Rooms* was published by Test Centre in 2018. He is Senior Lecturer in Creative Writing at Goldsmiths, University of London.

Ian Willms is a Canadian photographer whose practice lies between traditional photojournalism and contemporary photography. In 'Why We Walk', Willms traced the journey of his Mennonite ancestors fleeing persecution in 1920s Russia across Europe to Canada.

Jonathan Wright is a British literary translator who has translated more than a dozen Arabic novels and short-story collections into English since 2008, including three winners of the International Prize for Arabic Fiction. He has won the Banipal Prize for Arabic Literary Translation twice.

Che Yeun's short stories have been published in *Virginia Quarterly Review* and *Kenyon Review* online. She works as a Historian of Science and Medicine, and lives in Boston.

Jay G. Ying is a poet, fiction writer, critic and translator based in Edinburgh. His debut poetry pamphlet, *Wedding Beasts*, was published in 2019. A second pamphlet, *Katabasis*, forthcoming in 2020, has been awarded a New Poets Prize. He is a contributing editor at the *White Review*.